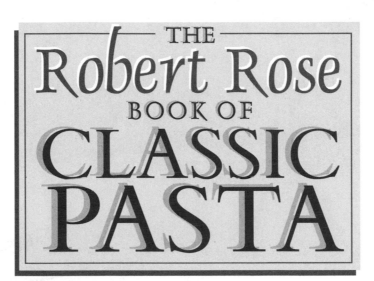

# THE Robert Rose BOOK OF CLASSIC PASTA

# THE
# Robert Rose
## BOOK OF
# CLASSIC
# PASTA

**Robert**
**ROSE**

# THE ROBERT ROSE BOOK OF CLASSIC PASTA

**For complete cataloguing data, see page 6.**

| | |
|---|---|
| DESIGN AND PAGE COMPOSITION: | MATTHEWS COMMUNICATIONS DESIGN |
| PHOTOGRAPHY: | MARK T. SHAPIRO |
| ART DIRECTION, FOOD PHOTOGRAPHY: | DON FERNLEY |
| FOOD STYLIST: | KATE BUSH |
| MANAGING EDITOR: | PETER MATTHEWS |
| RECIPE EDITOR: | LELEIGH LANDRY |
| INDEXER: | BARBARA SCHON |
| COLOR SCANS & FILM: | POINTONE GRAPHICS |

*Cover photo: (PASTA PRIMAVERA, PAGE 34)*

Distributed in the U.S. by:
Firefly Books (U.S.) Inc.
P.O. Box 1338
Ellicott Station
Buffalo, NY    14205

Distributed in Canada by:
Stoddart Publishing Co. Ltd.
34 Lesmill Road
North York, Ontario
M3B 2T6

*ORDER LINES*
Tel: (416) 499-8412
Fax: (416) 499-8313

*ORDER LINES*
Tel: (416) 445-3333
Fax: (416) 445-5967

Published by:   Robert Rose Inc. • 156 Duncan Mill Road, Suite 12
Toronto, Ontario, Canada  M3B 2N2   Tel: (416) 449-3535

Printed in Canada

1234567 BP 00 99 98 97

# Contents

**Canadian Cataloguing in Publication Data**

The Robert Rose book of classic pasta

Includes index.

ISBN 1-896503-03-9

1. Cookery (Pasta).    I. Title.    II. Title: Classic pasta.

TX809.M17R457 1997        641.8'22        C97-930565-9

**Photo Prop Credits**

The publisher expresses appreciation to the following suppliers of props used in the food photography appearing in this book:

| | |
|---|---|
| THAMES VALLEY BRICK AND TILE, TORONTO | TILES, GLASSBLOCK |
| VILLEROY AND BOSCH LTD., TORONTO | TABLEWARE |
| GRANT'S FINE CHINA AND GIFTS, TORONTO | TABLEWARE |
| JUNORS, TORONTO | TABLEWARE |
| B.B. BARGOON'S, TORONTO | LINENS |

# Introduction

When we first developed the idea of publishing *The Robert Rose Book of Classic Pasta*, we were inspired by two factors.

The first was the continuing demand for this book's predecessor, *Rose Reisman Brings Home Pasta Dishes*, which has been unavailable for several years. The concept of the book — to select over 125 pasta dishes from top North American restaurants and adapt them for home cooking — clearly had appeal. So we revised the recipes to make them even easier to follow, with larger type, metric equivalents for all measurements, and simple step-by-step instructions.

The second factor was (and is) the enduring popularity of pasta itself. It's simple, yet remarkably versatile. It's inexpensive. Pasta also provides an excellent source of carbohydrates which, combined with meat, poultry, fish, seafood, vegetables and/or cheese, serves as the basis for a complete, nutritious meal.

Pasta can be anything you want it to be. It's an amazingly simple food consisting mainly of flour, water, and eggs. Other ingredients, such as tomatoes, spinach and herbs, can be added to the dough for extra flavor and color. It can be prepared with tomato sauce as a simple dish, or added to for a more substantial meal. And the ever-popular macaroni and cheese is always popular with children of all ages.

This book features over 125 pasta dishes selected from the menus of 48 top-rated restaurants. A special selection of low-fat, low-calorie recipes have also been included, and all recipes have been thoroughly tested in adapting them for the home kitchen. Most can be prepared in less than 30 minutes, and the ingredients are easy to find at local supermarkets.

Enjoy your classic pasta!

— *The Editors of Robert Rose*

# Making Perfect Pasta

1.  Cook pasta in a large pot of boiling water. Use 12 to 16 cups (3 to 4 L) water for each pound (500 g) of pasta. Add a little oil to prevent pasta from sticking. Stir pasta occasionally while cooking.

2.  Cook pasta *al dente*, or firm to the bite. Never overcook or it will become soft and lose all its texture. When cooked, drain in colander, then transfer to a serving dish. If pasta is to be eaten right away, add sauce immediately and toss. If not, add a little sauce, water or chicken stock (so pasta does not stick), then cover and set aside. Do not add sauce to pasta until just ready to serve, or pasta will absorb the sauce, leaving the appearance of not enough.

3.  Prepare the sauce while the pasta is cooking. Plan ahead so the sauce will be completed at the same time the pasta is cooked.

4.  For these recipes, 1/2 lb (250 g) dry pasta serves 4 people, 3/4 lb (375 g) serves 6 people, and 1 lb (500 g) serves 8 people.

5.  You can prepare the pasta early in the day if necessary. Drain cooked pasta, rinse with cold water and add 3 tbsp (45 mL) of stock or 3 tbsp (45 mL) of the sauce to be used, or 3 tbsp (45 mL) of the water in which the pasta was cooked. (This will ensure that pasta strands do not stick.) Let sit at room temperature. Before serving, either warm slightly in a microwave for 1 minute at High (be careful not to overcook the pasta), or heat sauce well and pour over pasta immediately.

6.  Heavier pasta such as rigatoni or jumbo shells need a heavier, more robust sauce. Lighter pasta such as fettuccine, linguine or spaghetti need a finer sauce and more finely diced vegetables. Sauces for rotini or penne should be somewhere between fine and robust.

7.  Homemade pastas can be delicious (see page 21 for information on making fresh pasta), but most of the time we use dried pasta. There are several reasons for this:
    - It is easier to find, store, and costs much less than fresh.

- It lacks the fat and cholesterol of the fresh types, which have eggs added.

- There are more varieties of dried pasta readily available.

- Dried pastas have consistent flavor and texture. Fresh pasta can stick, even if cooked properly, and is best only if cooked immediately after the pasta is made.

- It can be stored at room temperature for up to 1 year.

8. If reheating leftover pasta, add more stock or tomato sauce to provide extra moisture.

# The Complete Pasta Pantry

There are a number of key ingredients that you'll find useful to have on hand for the recipes in this book.

## ARTICHOKES

You can use canned, drained artichokes or cook your own. If using fresh artichokes, cook them in boiling, salted water or a dry white wine that has been flavored with herbs and oil. Cook just until tender, approximately 30 minutes, for larger hearts. Test doneness by pulling off an outer leaf. If it pulls off easily, the artichoke is ready. Peel off leaves until you reach the heart.

## BUTTER OR MARGARINE

In this book butter or margarine can be used interchangeably, depending on one's preference. Butter is a saturated (animal) fat, and therefore contains cholesterol. Margarine has no cholesterol, and is not a saturated fat. Both contain similar amounts of fat and calories.

Unsalted butter has a fresher and healthier taste. It can be kept frozen so that you can always have it on hand. If cholesterol is a concern, substitute a good-quality vegetable margarine.

## CHEESES

There is no "perfect" cheese for a specific pasta dish. The recipes give recommendations, but feel free to substitute. If you feel the taste of a cheese is too strong, substitute a milder cheese and vice versa. Below is a list of common cheeses used with pasta.

### The Best Hard Cheeses for Grating

**Parmesan** is probably the most common cheese used with pasta. It is always better to buy it fresh and grate it yourself. If you need grated cheese on hand, most groceries have a deli department where they sell it freshly grated. The packaged grated cheese is not as fresh and does not always contain the best parmigiana cheeses. Parmesan should have a good golden color, which indicates a younger cheese. The best Parmesan will be labeled "Parmigiano-Reggiano."

Either grated or whole, Parmesan cheese can be stored for long periods in the refrigerator. If storing in whole pieces, wrap each piece tightly with plastic wrap and then with foil; this will keep for several months. Grate these just before serving.

**Asiago**. A hard, dry cheese with a strong flavor.

**Aged Provolone**. A pear-shaped cheese. The aging gives it a strong taste.

**Aged Gouda**. Hard and tasty.

**Romano**. Very sharp and salty. If you do not like the taste, substitute Parmesan.

## Soft Cheeses

**Blue Cheeses**. These include Roquefort, Gorgonzola, Danish Blue, and Stilton. Soft and creamy with a blue mold. Very distinctive flavor. They are usually used in combination with a milder cheese.

**Cottage Cheese**. White, soft curds; can be used interchangeably with Ricotta cheese. Use 2% cottage cheese for the best flavor and texture.

**Cream Cheese**. Soft and creamy. Ricotta or cottage cheese can be substituted, or light cream cheese (with 25% fewer calories) can be used.

**Goat Cheese (chevre)**. Distinctive flavor, made from goat's milk. When wrapped tightly, will keep for 3 to 4 weeks in the refrigerator.

**Mascarpone**. A delicious double cream, soft and creamy Italian cheese usually used in Tiramisu, an Italian dessert. Can be substituted for ricotta or cream cheese.

**Ricotta**. Creamy and bland. Use in place of cottage cheese, cream cheese or mascarpone cheese. Ricotta comes in 5% or 10% fat. Either can be used. Read expiry date on package container. This cheese can usually be kept for 7 to 10 days.

## Semi-Soft Cheeses

**Brie**. Soft, mild and sweet cheese.

**Emmentaler**. Type of Swiss cheese. Firm texture with a pleasant, nutty flavor.

**Fontina**. Creamy and buttery whole-fat cheese. Any mild cheese can be substituted.

**Havarti**. Mild and sweet. Any mild cheese can be substituted.

**Gruyere**. A type of Swiss cheese with a tasty, delicate flavor. Sweeter than Emmentaler.

**Jarlsberg**. Nutty, Swiss-like flavor. An excellent cheese for cooking or eating.

**Mozzarella**. Creamy, mild, and sweet. Can be kept for 2 to 3 weeks if wrapped tightly. This cheese can be replaced with low-fat versions because of its mild taste.

**Monterey Jack**. Soft and mild. Any mild cheese can be substituted.

**Muenster**. Creamy and bland. Any creamy, mild cheese can be substituted.

## CHICKEN AND MEAT

Meat recipes generally call for quantities of 1/2 to 3/4 lb (250 to 375 g). These include: ground beef, chicken or veal; boneless, skinless chicken breast; lean steak; boneless pork; stewing beef or veal; spicy and sweet sausages.

## FISH AND SEAFOOD

If desired, you can interchange fish and seafood ingredients in most recipes. Buy fresh where possible, although frozen ingredients work well, too. Keep in mind that shellfish freeze better than fish fillets. Shrimps, scallops or squid, when well wrapped, can be kept in the freezer for up to 2 months.

Canned clams are extremely useful to have on hand, since they make a good seafood sauce if fresh fish is unavailable. The liquid can be used as a seafood stock.

## GARLIC

Fresh, whole, firm heads of garlic are always the best to use. Stored in a cool, dry, airy spot, they will stay fresh for 2 to 3 weeks. Garlic powder or salt should not be used if a true garlic taste is required. Chopped garlic, packed in a jar of oil, can be quite good (refrigerate after opening). Still, the fullest garlic flavor comes only from fresh cloves.

## HERBS

Fresh herbs such as basil, coriander (also called Chinese parsley), dill, parsley and oregano are most commonly used for pasta dishes. Fresh herbs are almost always preferable to dried. (The exception is for sauces that require longer cooking times, in which case dried herbs provide a more intense flavor.)

When fresh herbs are not in season, use dried herbs. Be sure to keep them in airtight jars, stored in a cool, dry place.

Good dried herbs to keep on hand include basil, oregano, dill, chili powder, chili flakes and cayenne pepper.

The recipes in this book include measurements for both fresh and dried herbs. A good rule to follow is 1/2 tsp (2 mL) of dried for 1 tbsp (15 mL) of fresh herbs.

## MISCELLANEOUS ESSENTIALS

**Beans.** Keep a good variety of canned beans on hand, including red and white kidney beans, chick peas and black beans. These are great in pasta salads and soups.

**Black olives.** Canned, pitted black olives are easy to measure and can be used in a number of pasta dishes.

**Oriental ingredients.** These are handy to have for Asian pasta dishes: rice wine vinegar, hoisin sauce, soya sauce, sesame oil, oyster sauce and ginger root (fresh or marinated in oil).

**Pine nuts.** Store in freezer and toast before use. Toast either in 400°F (200°C) oven for 10 to 15 minutes until golden or on top of oven in skillet for 2 to 3 minutes.

## MUSHROOMS

Regular white mushrooms are called for in many recipes, but you can substitute wild mushrooms such as oyster, cremini, portobello or shiitake. They give an exotic flavor and texture to the pasta dish and are well worth the extra expense. Many groceries now carry a variety of different mushrooms.

Dried mushrooms can also be used. They should be soaked in approximately 1 cup (250 mL) of warm water or stock for 30 minutes. Drain well before using. Usually, 1 oz (30 g) of dry mushrooms equals 1/2 lb (250 g) of fresh.

## OIL

Vegetable or olive oil is specified in each recipe. Canola oil is the best vegetable oil to use.

For olive oil, the "first pressed" or "extra virgin" varieties are best because of their rich, fruity consistency. The first pressing is important because the oil has not been heated and is free from chemical additives. The darker the oil, the richer the olive taste. If the flavor is too strong for you, high-quality lighter oils are available and provide a more subtle taste. Oils labeled "cold-pressed" are good when you want the olive taste to be dominant, or if dipping bread.

The least expensive olive oil is labeled "pure olive oil," and is made from the second or third pressings. This can be used as a substitute for other vegetable oils, when the taste of olive oil is not important.

Both vegetable and olive oils should be stored in dark, cool places for 1 1/2 to 2 years. After opening, use within 8 to 12 weeks.

## STOCK

For chicken, beef, vegetable and seafood stock, try to find the time to make your own. It's simple and yields the best results.

In 12 cups (3 L) of water, boil a variety of vegetables such as carrots, onions and celery with your favorite dried herbs and spices. For chicken, meat or fish stocks, add 2 lbs (1 kg) of chicken, beef or fish bones, and simmer for 2 hours. Strain the liquid and use immediately, or freeze for up to 2 months.

If homemade stock is unavailable, use canned broth. Otherwise, use bouillon powders or cubes for chicken or beef stock (1 tsp [5 mL] added to 1 cup [250 mL] of hot water). Keep in mind, however, that these substitutes can be high in sodium.

Bottled clam juice or liquid from canned clams makes a good substitute for fish broth.

## TOMATOES

Many of the recipes call for chopped or crushed tomatoes. When in season, fresh, ripe plum tomatoes are best. Do not ripen tomatoes in direct sunlight. Place them in a paper bag and leave in indirect sunlight. Chop them and try to save the juice for the sauce.

Canned tomatoes. When tomatoes are not in season, it is better to use canned tomatoes, preferably Italian plum. Use whole and break up with back of spoon while cooking. For crushed tomatoes, place contents of can in food processor; switch on and off quickly until desired consistency is achieved.

Try not to use canned tomato sauce or seasoned tomatoes because the seasoning is not fresh, and the salt content is very high.

Tomato paste, a concentrated form of tomatoes, adds great flavor to sauces. It also helps to thicken the sauce. Buy small cans of paste. Refrigerate after opening, or freeze in small containers.

Tomato concentrate comes in a tube and is twice as intense as tomato paste. It has a better flavor than paste and leaves no bitter aftertaste.

Sun-dried tomatoes are available packaged dry or in bulk, or packed in oil. Pour boiling water over dry tomatoes and let soften for 15 minutes. Drain, then use. Use dry for less fat and calories.

## VEGETABLES

A wide range of vegetables are used in these recipes. Most will keep for at least a week in the proper section of the refrigerator. In addition to tomatoes and mushrooms (discussed separately in this section), some that you may want to keep on hand include: green, red and/or yellow sweet bell peppers; red, white and yellow onions; carrots; zucchini; eggplant; broccoli; snow peas; green onions; potatoes and yams; and, in the freezer, sweet green peas and chopped spinach.

## VINEGARS

Balsamic vinegar provides the mildest, sweetest taste. Other vinegars to have on hand include those made from rice wine and red wine.

# Pasta Glossary

There are so many varieties of fresh and dry pasta that it is easy to be confused about which type to match with a particular sauce. Some master pasta chefs have strict guidelines, but pasta is flexible — in more ways than one! — so feel free to combine whatever pasta you like with a sauce that suits you.

That being said, thicker or stuffed pastas are generally better with robust sauces, while thin-strand pastas are best with lighter sauces. With special pastas such as bow-ties or wheels, lighter sauces may be preferable since they will not obscure the shapes. Whichever pasta you choose, be sure to get the best quality you can — whether fresh or dried pasta.

Store-bought fresh pasta should be stored in the refrigerator up to the date on package. Homemade pasta should be used immediately or stored in the refrigerator for up to 2 days. Homemade dried pasta can be stored for 7 days in the refrigerator.

Dried pasta can be stored either in its original packaging or in an airtight container for up to 1 year. Here it's worth remembering that a good dry pasta is always better than stale "fresh" pasta.

With these points in mind, here's a list of some of the more common dry pastas. All of them can be found in grocery stores.

**Agnolotti** — Similar to ravioli, usually semicircular or square in shape. It is filled with various ingredients such as cheese, meat, or vegetables. You can substitute any stuffed pasta, such as ravioli or tortellini.

**Angel Hair** — *See* Capelli d'Angelo.

**Bow-Ties** — *See* Farfalle.

**Cannelloni** — Usually sold fresh as 4- by 5-inch (9 by 12 cm) flat pieces or as a dried pasta in rolled form. They can be filled with meat or cheese fillings and are usually baked in a sauce. They are smaller than manicotti, but can be used interchangeably with them. Use about 1 tbsp (15 mL) of filling in each.

**Capelli d'Angelo (Angel Hair)** — Very thin strands of pasta, usually sold in coils.

**Capellini** — Similar to angel hair pasta, but slightly thicker.

**Conchiglie (Shells)** — Shaped like conch shells, ranging in size from small bite-size pasta to large shells that can be stuffed with meat, cheese, or vegetable fillings.

**Farfalle (Bow–Ties)** — Shaped like bow–ties — or butterflies, if you like — they come in a variety of sizes. Most often used in the same way as a wide, flat noodle.

**Fettuccine (Tagliatelle)** — Long, flat pasta , usually about 1/4 inch (5 mm) wide.

**Fusilli (Spirals, Rotini)** — Shaped like twisted spaghetti or corkscrews, about 3 inches (7 cm) in length.

**Gnocchi** — Dumpling-like in appearance, but nevertheless a type of pasta. Make your own and freeze them, or buy the packaged gnocchi, which are usually excellent. Gnocchi is made from potatoes and flour, and can be served with a variety of sauces.

**Lasagne** — Sheets of fresh or dried pasta, usually measuring 13 inches (30 cm) long by 3 inches (7 cm) wide; usually cooked, layered with filling and sauce, and baked.

**Linguine** — A flat, strand-type pasta, like fettuccine, but not as wide.

**Macaroni** — Available as long, relatively thin tubes, but are most familiar in "elbow" form — that is, as short, crescent-shaped tubes of pasta used for casseroles or soups.

**Manicotti** — A rolled pasta like cannelloni, but larger; usually filled with a cheese mixture and baked with a sauce. You can buy them in dried form, or buy sheets of lasagna and cut to desired size, usually 5 by 4 inches (12.5 by 10 cm). Use about 1 tbsp (15 mL) filling for each shell.

**Orzo** — Sometimes used as a substitute for rice, which it resembles, but is heavier and fuller. Good in soups.

**Penne Rigate** — Quill shaped, tubular pasta, cut diagonally; comes in various sizes, but most often measuring 2 inches (5 cm) in length. Good with heavier meat sauces.

**Radiatore** — An unusually shaped, bite-sized pasta, featuring fins like those of an old-fashioned hot water radiator.

**Ravioli** — Square pasta, 1 to 2 inches (2.5 to 5 cm) across, filled with a small amount of cheese or meat filling and crimped at the edges. You can prepare your own or buy ready-made frozen. Serve with a sauce.

**Rigatoni** — Large, ridged tubes of pasta, usually about 1 1/2 inches (3 cm) long. Excellent with a chunky sauce.

**Shells** — *See* Conchiglie

**Spaghetti** — Best known of all pastas, often used as a generic term for any strand-type pasta, ranging from thin capellini to thick spaghettoni.

**Spaghettini** — Thinner than spaghetti, but thicker than vermicelli.

**Tagliatelle** — *See* Fettuccine.

**Tortellini** — Similar to ravioli, but with a twisted, irregular shape; usually filled with cheese or meat. You can prepare your own or use ready-made. Fillings for this pasta are interchangeable with manicotti, cannelloni, or jumbo pasta shells.

**Vermicelli** — Thinner than spaghettini, but thicker than capellini.

**Wheels** — Circular,  bite-sized pasta with various configurations of "hubs" and "spokes." Good in salads and soups.

**Ziti** — A tubular pasta similar to penne.

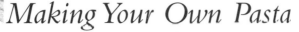

# *Making Your Own Pasta*

As pasta has grown in popularity, many people have started to make their own pasta. It takes time and patience, but for the true pasta gourmet, it is well worth the effort.

| | BASIC PASTA DOUGH | |
|---|---|---|
| | MAKES 3 TO 4 SERVINGS, APPROXIMATELY 12 OZ (375 G) | |
| 2 | large eggs | 2 |
| 2 tsp | oil | 10 mL |
| 1 1/2 cups | all-purpose flour | 375 mL |
| Pinch | salt | Pinch |

1. In a bowl beat eggs and oil. Sift the flour and salt over the eggs. Mix with a fork and form into a ball. If it is too sticky, add some flour until it is easy to handle. If too dry, add some water.

2. Knead for approximately 8 minutes, until smooth. Wrap in a slightly moistened towel and let rest approximately 30 minutes on the counter before rolling and cutting into various pasta shapes.

   If using a food processor or electric mixer, add flour and salt to bowl; with motor running, add the eggs and oil. Mix until the dough becomes a ball. If too sticky, add more flour; if too dry, add a few drops of water. Knead for approximately 5 minutes until smooth. Let rest for 30 minutes.

   The classic way of making pasta is to sift the flour and salt together, mounding it on a table. Make a well in the center of the mound and break the eggs into it. Add oil. With a fork begin to gather the flour slowly from the sides into the middle until all is incorporated. Follow the same kneading directions as above.

| | PASTA VARIATIONS | |
|---|---|---|

Some flavorful and colorful variations to the pasta can be added quite simply. Just add the following ingredients and continue with the same method of making the basic pasta dough.

### *Tomato Pasta*

Add 2 tbsp (25 mL) tomato paste to basic pasta dough. Add more flour if too sticky.

### Green Pasta (Pasta Verdi)

Make basic pasta dough using only one egg. Add 8 oz (250 g) finely chopped, cooked spinach, well drained. If dough is too wet, add extra flour.

### Herb Pasta

Chop 2 tbsp (25 mL) of any herb of your choice, and add to basic pasta dough.

### Whole Wheat Pasta

Use 1 cup (250 mL) whole wheat flour and 1/4 cup (50 mL) white flour in place of white flour in the basic pasta dough recipe. Note that this produces a heavier pasta. For a lighter version, substitute half whole wheat flour and half white flour.

### Black Pepper Pasta

Add 2 tsp (10 mL) freshly ground black pepper to basic recipe.

### Garlic Pasta

Finely chop 5 cloves of garlic and add to basic pasta dough along with 1 tbsp (15 mL) water.

### Semolina Pasta

This is often considered to be the best-tasting of all types of pasta dough. Substitute semolina flour for all-purpose flour in basic pasta dough. You may find the dough very hard to knead, however, and it can tend to clog the holes of electric machines. So use with care.

### Black Pasta

Use only 1 egg in basic pasta dough. Mix 2 tbsp (25 mL) squid ink with 1/4 cup (50 mL) water. Combine ink mixture with the other ingredients and proceed in the usual manner.

## ROLLING THE DOUGH

### Rolling Pasta by Hand

- A long rolling pin and fairly large working space is essential. Work quickly or the pasta will crack and dry.
- Roll the dough away from you, stretching it as you roll. After each roll, give the dough a quarter turn to keep the circular shape.

- If the dough is sticking to your working surface, dust it with a little flour. Pull and stretch the dough instead of rolling it. To stretch it, place the dough on top of the rolling pin and pull carefully.

- Once the dough covers a large area, let it hang over the counter to stretch more. In a few minutes the dough will look smooth and should be very thin, about 1/8 inch (2 mm) thick.

- If the dough is to be used for unfilled pasta, spread it on a towel to dry for approximately 30 minutes. Use it immediately for filled pasta such as ravioli or tortellini.

- Now the dough is ready to cut into shapes of your choice.

### PASTA MACHINES

Two types of wringer-style pasta machines are available. One has a motor and the other is turned by hand.

## Using a Manual Pasta Machine

- After the dough is rested, divide into 3 or 4 pieces. Keep the pieces not being used wrapped in plastic.

- Flatten a piece of dough with your hand just so that it will fit through the pasta machine at the widest setting. Feed the pasta into the machine with one hand while working the machine with the other hand.

- After the pasta comes out, fold it over and feed it again into the machine. When the dough begins to get smooth and elastic, start to narrow the roller openings. Continue this process until the dough achieves the desired thickness.

- Lay the pieces on a well-floured surface. If the dough is to sit for any length of time, cover it with a towel. Now attach the cutting attachment desired to the pasta machine. Follow the manufacturer's instructions.

- Sprinkle the freshly cut pasta with some flour. Toss in a pile, or gather in strands. Now you can lay the pasta on a drying rack. Alternatively, you can place it in the refrigerator, where it will stay fresh for up to 1 week, or in the freezer for up to 2 months.

## Electric Pasta Machines

An electric machine pushes the dough through a die that creates the desired pasta shape. Some of the more elaborate machines will also mix and knead the dough. After a few minutes, it comes out of the other end in various shapes, depending upon the attachment affixed.

The biggest problem with these machines is that the various attachments are easily clogged with flour, and the time cleaning them can be considerable.

## *Fettuccine (tagliatelle) or any flat noodle*

• Roll up the dough like a jelly roll and cut in even widths to desired shape, approximately 1/4 inch (5 mm) thick. Cook immediately or let dry for a few days before storing.

## *Manicotti, Cannelloni, Lasagne*

• Cut flat sheets of pasta to width and length desired. The most common size for manicotti or cannelloni is 4 by 5 inches (10 by 12.5 cm).

• In boiling water with a little oil added to prevent sticking, cook pasta for about 2 to 3 minutes. Do not place too many pieces in pot, or they may stick together. Drain and rinse with cold water.

• The pasta sheets can then be filled with meat, cheese or vegetable stuffing; later, they can be covered and baked with a sauce over top so the pasta does not dry out.

• To store the pasta sheets, layer them with plastic or wax paper. Fresh pasta is best cooked immediately, but can be stored in the refrigerator for up to 1 week, or in the freezer for as long as 2 months.

## *Ravioli and Tortellini*

• Prepare the desired filling and set aside. Roll the pasta dough into strips approximately 12 inches (30 cm) long and 4 inches (10 cm) wide. Keep unused strips covered with a damp towel.

• Brush each strip of dough with a little beaten egg. Place a small amount of filling (approximately 1/2 tsp [2 mL]) at  intervals of 1 1/2 inches (4 cm) on the pasta.

• Lay a second sheet over top and press down firmly. For square shapes, cut between the fillings with a knife, pastry wheel, or special pasta cutter.

• For round shapes, cut circles about 1 to 2 inches (2.5 to 5 cm) in diameter. For tortellini, cut 2-inch (5 cm) circles, and place a small amount of filling in one half of the circle. Fold the pasta and crimp the edges together.

# PASTA WITH *Cheese*

# *Four-Cheese Macaroni*

**SERVES 4 TO 6**

**TIP**

Experiment with whatever cheeses you have on hand; Monterey Jack, Fontina, Provolone and goat cheese all melt well and Romano and Asiago provide a bite similar to Parmesan.

| | | |
|---|---|---|
| 8 oz | mozzarella cheese | 250 g |
| 4 oz | Cheddar cheese | 125 g |
| 4 oz | Swiss cheese, preferably Gruyere | 125 g |
| 3/4 cup | grated Parmesan cheese | 175 mL |
| 12 oz | elbow macaroni | 375 g |
| 1/4 cup | melted butter | 50 mL |
| | Salt and pepper to taste | |

1. Finely dice 4 oz (125 g) of the mozzarella, 2 oz (50 g) of the Cheddar and 2 oz (50 g) of the Swiss cheese; combine diced cheeses.

2. Grate remaining mozzarella, Cheddar and Swiss cheese; combine grated cheeses with Parmesan.

3. In a large pot of boiling salted water, cook elbow macaroni for 8 to 10 minutes or until *al dente*; drain. Toss with all the diced cheese, half the grated cheese and 2 tbsp (25 mL) of the melted butter; mix well. Season to taste with salt and pepper.

4. Sprinkle remaining grated cheese on top, drizzle with remaining butter and serve immediately.

*— Riviera —*
*New Orleans*

# *Penne with Bell Peppers, Mushrooms and Cheese*

**SERVES 6 TO 8 AS AN APPETIZER**

**TIP**

To toast pine nuts, bake in 350° F (180° C) oven about 8 minutes or until golden and fragrant.

Substitute spinach for the arugula.

Try any soft, mild cheese — such as Havarti or brick — instead of provolone.

**Preheat broiler**

| | | |
|---|---|---|
| 2 | peppers, any color | 2 |
| 2 tbsp | olive oil | 25 mL |
| 2 | cloves garlic, crushed | 2 |
| 1 cup | chopped mushrooms | 250 mL |
| 1/2 cup | sliced onions | 125 mL |
| 1 | green onion, chopped | 1 |
| 2/3 cup | chicken stock | 150 mL |
| 2 tbsp | dry white wine | 25 mL |
| 1 1/2 cups | whipping (35%) cream | 375 mL |
| 1 tsp | minced anchovies | 5 mL |
| 1 cup | grated provolone cheese | 250 mL |
| 1/2 cup | grated Parmesan cheese | 125 mL |
| 1 lb | penne | 500 g |
| 1/4 cup | butter | 50 mL |
| 1/2 cup | toasted pine nuts | 125 mL |
| 2 oz | arugula, washed and chopped | 50 g |

1. Broil peppers in oven for 15 minutes or until charred, turning often. Cool. Peel skins, remove stem and seeds and cut into strips; set aside.

2. In a skillet heat oil over medium-high heat. Cook garlic, mushrooms, onions and green onion until golden brown, stirring frequently. Stir in chicken stock and white wine; cook until slightly reduced, about 2 minutes. Stir in cream and anchovies; cook until slightly thickened, about 5 minutes. Stir in cheeses; blend well.

3. In a blender or food processor, purée sauce. Strain sauce over skillet and put over low heat to keep warm.

4. In large pot of boiling salted water cook penne 8 to 10 minutes or until *al dente*; drain.

5. Stir butter into sauce until it melts. Toss pasta with sauce, pepper strips, pine nuts and arugula. Serve immediately.

— *Scoozi* —
*Chicago*

# *Penne with Tomatoes, Black Olives and Goat Cheese*

SERVES 4

**TIP**

Spice this up by adding more hot pepper flakes.

| | | |
|---|---|---|
| 1 tbsp | olive oil | 15 mL |
| 1 | clove garlic, minced | 1 |
| 1 cup | chopped onions | 250 mL |
| 1 | can (28 oz [796 mL]) Italian plum tomatoes, with juice | 1 |
| 12 oz | penne | 375 g |
| 3 oz | goat cheese, crumbled | 75 g |
| 1/2 cup | sliced black olives | 125 mL |
| Pinch | hot pepper flakes | Pinch |
| | Salt and pepper to taste | |
| 1/4 cup | grated Parmesan cheese | 50 mL |

1. In a large saucepan, heat olive oil over medium–high heat. Add garlic and onions; cook 4 minutes or until softened. Stir in tomatoes, breaking them up with the back of a spoon. Reduce heat to medium-low and cook until thickened, about 10 minutes.

2. Meanwhile, in a large pot of boiling salted water, cook penne 8 to 10 minutes or until *al dente*; drain.

3. Stir goat cheese, olives and hot pepper flakes into sauce; toss with pasta. Season to taste with salt and pepper. Serve immediately, sprinkled with Parmesan cheese.

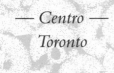

— *Centro* —
*Toronto*

# PASTA WITH *Vegetables*

# Fettuccine with Artichokes

**SERVES 4 TO 6**

**TIP**

Instead of canned, drained artichoke hearts, cook your own. Trim the leaves and choke from 5 artichokes. Thinly slice hearts. In a saucepan melt 1 tbsp (15 mL) butter over medium-low heat; cook sliced artichoke hearts, covered, until tender when pierced with the tip of a knife, about 10 minutes.

| | | |
|---|---|---|
| 12 oz | fettuccine | 375 g |
| 1/4 cup | butter | 50 mL |
| 2 | cloves garlic, crushed | 2 |
| 1 | can (14 oz [398 mL]) artichoke hearts, drained and quartered | 1 |
| 1/4 cup | dry white wine | 50 mL |
| 1 1/4 cups | whipping (35%) cream | 300 mL |
| 1/2 cup | grated Parmesan cheese | 50 mL |
| | Salt and pepper to taste | |

1. In a large pot of boiling salted water, cook fettuccine 8 to 10 minutes or until *al dente*. Meanwhile, prepare the sauce.

2. In a large skillet, melt butter over medium-high heat. Add garlic and cook until light brown. Stir in artichoke hearts and white wine; cook 2 minutes. Stir in cream; cook until cream begins to bubble, about 3 minutes. Add drained pasta and Parmesan; toss until cheese melts. Season to taste with salt and pepper. Serve immediately.

*Umberto al Porto*
*Vancouver*

# Pasta Salad with Roasted Peppers and Onions

**SERVES 4 TO 6**

**TIP**

Use light sour cream to reduce the fat.

**Preheat broiler**

| | | |
|---|---|---|
| 6 | red or yellow peppers (or a combination) | 6 |
| 12 oz | small shell pasta or ditali | 375 g |
| 1/4 cup | olive oil | 50 mL |
| 3 | onions, sliced | 3 |
| 1 tbsp | crushed garlic | 15 mL |
| 2 tsp | paprika | 10 mL |
| 3 | tomatoes, diced | 3 |
| 1 1/4 cups | sour cream | 300 mL |
| Dash | hot sauce | Dash |
| | Salt and pepper to taste | |

1. Broil peppers in oven, turning often, for 15 minutes or until charred. Cool. Peel skins, remove stem and seeds, and cut into strips; set aside.

2. In a large pot of boiling salted water, cook pasta 8 to 10 minutes or until *al dente*. Meanwhile, prepare sauce.

3. In a large skillet, heat oil over high heat. Add onions and cook, stirring frequently, until golden brown. Stir in garlic and paprika; cook 1 minute. Stir in tomatoes and pepper strips; cook 1 minute longer. Remove from heat.

4. Toss drained pasta with sauce, sour cream and hot sauce. Season to taste with salt and pepper. Serve immediately.

*City Restaurant*
*Los Angeles*

# Fettuccine with Mushrooms in a Creamy Tomato Sauce

**SERVES 4 TO 5**

**TIP**

This is an extra-special dish made with wild mushrooms, or part cultivated and part wild mushrooms. Use oyster, porcini or chanterelles — or a combination.

For an extra lemon lift, add 1 tsp (5 mL) grated lemon zest along with the lemon juice.

| | | |
|---|---|---|
| 12 oz | fettuccine | 375 g |
| 3 tbsp | butter | 45 mL |
| 1 lb | mushrooms (preferably wild), sliced | 500 g |
| 2 tbsp | crushed garlic | 25 mL |
| 1 1/4 cups | whipping (35%) cream | 300 mL |
| 1/2 cup | diced tomatoes | 125 mL |
| 2 tsp | freshly squeezed lemon juice | 10 mL |
| 1/3 cup | grated Parmesan cheese | 75 mL |
| | Salt and pepper to taste | |

1. In a large pot of boiling salted water, cook fettuccine 8 to 10 minutes or until *al dente*. Meanwhile, prepare the sauce.

2. In a large saucepan, melt butter over high heat. Add mushrooms and garlic; cook, stirring, 3 minutes. Stir in cream and cook about 3 minutes. Reduce heat to medium; stir in tomatoes and lemon juice. Add drained pasta and Parmesan; toss. Season to taste with salt and pepper. Serve immediately.

*City Restaurant*
*Los Angeles*

PENNE WITH BELL PEPPERS, MUSHROOMS AND CHEESE (PAGE 27) ➤

# Spicy Fettuccine with Sweet Peppers

**SERVES 4 TO 5**

**TIP**

Make this when tomatoes and peppers are at their peak season.

Use any combination of peppers if these are not available.

Vary the hotness by increasing or reducing the quantity of hot pepper flakes.

| | | |
|---|---|---:|
| 1/3 cup | olive oil | 75 mL |
| 1/2 cup | finely chopped onions | 125 mL |
| 2 | cloves garlic, chopped | 2 |
| 1/4 tsp | hot pepper flakes, or to taste | 1 mL |
| 1/2 | green pepper, cut into thin strips | 1/2 |
| 1/2 | red pepper, cut into thin strips | 1/2 |
| 1/2 | yellow pepper, cut into thin strips | 1/2 |
| 4 | tomatoes, chopped | 4 |
| 12 oz | fettuccine | 375 g |
| 3/4 cup | grated Parmesan cheese | 175 mL |
| 2 tbsp | butter | 25 mL |
| | Salt to taste | |

1.  In a saucepan heat oil over medium–high heat. Add onions, garlic and hot pepper flakes; cook until golden brown. Increase heat to high. Stir in pepper strips and tomatoes; cook, stirring, until peppers wilt. Reduce heat to medium-low, cover and cook 20 minutes.
2.  Meanwhile, in a large pot of boiling salted water, cook fettuccine 8 to 10 minutes or until *al dente*; drain.
3.  Toss pasta with sauce. Stir in Parmesan and butter. Season to taste with salt. Serve immediately.

*Carlo's Restaurant*
*San Rafael*

◄ PASTA PRIMAVERA (PAGE 34)

# Pasta Primavera

**TIP**

For extra flavor, toast pine nuts in a 350° F (180° C) oven about 8 minutes or until golden and fragrant.

| | | |
|---|---|---|
| 12 oz | linguine | 375 g |
| 1 1/2 cups | chopped broccoli | 375 mL |
| 1 1/2 cups | snow peas | 375 mL |
| 1 cup | green peas | 250 mL |
| 1 cup | sliced zucchini | 250 mL |
| 6 | asparagus spears, cut in pieces | 6 |
| 1 tbsp | olive oil | 15 mL |
| 1 | tomato, diced | 1 |
| 1/4 cup | chopped fresh parsley | 50 mL |
| 1/2 tsp | minced garlic | 2 mL |
| 2 tbsp | olive oil | 25 mL |
| 1 3/4 cups | sliced mushrooms | 425 mL |
| 1 tsp | minced garlic | 5 mL |
| | Salt and pepper to taste | |
| 1 cup | whipping (35%) cream, warmed | 250 mL |
| 1/2 cup | grated Parmesan cheese | 125 mL |
| 1/3 cup | chopped fresh basil (or 1 1/2 tsp [7 mL] dried) | 75 mL |
| 1/3 cup | melted butter | 75 mL |
| 1/3 cup | pine nuts | 75 mL |

1. In a large pot of boiling salted water, cook linguine 8 to 10 minutes or until *al dente*. Meanwhile, prepare the sauce.

2. In a pot of boiling water, blanch broccoli, snow peas, green peas, zucchini and asparagus 2 minutes; refresh in cold water and drain. Set aside.

3. In a skillet heat 1 tbsp (15 mL) olive oil over medium heat. Add tomato, parsley and 1/2 tsp (2 mL) minced garlic; cook until tomato is softened, about 3 minutes; set aside.

*— Giuliano's —*
*Carmel*

4. In a large saucepan, heat olive oil over medium-high heat. Cook mushrooms and garlic until tender. Stir in green vegetables and tomato mixture; cook until heated through. Season to taste with salt and pepper.

5. Toss drained pasta with vegetable sauce, warmed cream, Parmesan, basil, butter and pine nuts. Serve immediately.

# Penne with Zucchini and Eggplant

**SERVES 4**

**TIP**

To peel tomatoes, blanch in boiling water for 30 seconds, drain, and cool under cold running water. Using a knife, peel skin off and discard. To seed, cut peeled tomato in half horizontally; with a small spoon, scoop out seeds and discard.

| | | |
|---|---|---|
| 12 oz | penne | 375 g |
| 1/3 cup | olive oil | 75 mL |
| 1 | clove garlic, crushed | 1 |
| 8 oz | eggplant, cut in julienne strips | 250 g |
| 7 oz | zucchini, cut in julienne strips | 210 g |
| 1 | large tomato, peeled, seeded and diced | 1 |
| 2 tbsp | chopped fresh basil (or 1 tsp [5 mL] dried) | 25 mL |
| 5 oz | mozzarella cheese, preferably smoked, finely diced | 150 g |
| | Salt and pepper to taste | |

1. In a large pot of boiling salted water, cook penne 8 to 10 minutes or until *al dente*. Meanwhile, prepare the sauce.

2. In a skillet heat oil over medium-high heat. Add garlic and cook until golden brown. Stir in eggplant and zucchini; cook 3 minutes. Stir in diced tomato and basil; cook 4 minutes longer. Add drained pasta and mix well. Stir in cheese; cook, stirring, until cheese begins to melt. Season to taste with salt and pepper. Serve immediately.

*The Blue Fox*
*San Francisco*

# Spaghettini with Sun-Dried Tomatoes

**SERVES 4 TO 6**

**TIP**

For extra flavor, toast pine nuts in a 350° F (180° C) oven about 8 minutes or until golden and fragrant.

It's more economical to buy dry-packed sun-dried tomatoes and rehydrate them yourself than to buy oil-packed. To rehydrate, bring a pan of water to a boil, add sun-dried tomatoes, reduce heat and simmer 5 minutes. Drain and use immediately, or put in a jar, add olive oil to cover, and refrigerate for later use.

| | | |
|---|---|---|
| 1 lb | spaghettini | 500 g |
| 1 tbsp | olive oil | 15 mL |
| 3 tbsp | minced garlic | 45 mL |
| 3 cups | chopped tomatoes | 750 mL |
| 3/4 cup | chopped, drained sun-dried tomatoes, packed in oil | 175 mL |
| 1/2 cup | chopped fresh basil (or 1 tbsp [15 mL] dried) | 125 mL |
| 1/2 cup | pine nuts | 125 mL |
| 1 cup | chicken stock | 250 mL |
| | Salt and pepper to taste | |

1. In a large pot of boiling salted water, cook spaghettini 8 to 10 minutes or until *al dente*. Meanwhile, prepare the sauce.
2. In a large saucepan, heat olive oil over medium-high heat. Add garlic and cook until golden brown. Stir in tomatoes, sun-dried tomatoes, basil and pine nuts; cook 3 minutes, stirring. Stir in chicken stock; cook 3 minutes longer. Season to taste with salt and pepper.
3. Toss drained pasta with sauce. Serve immediately.

*— Anthony's —*
*Houston*

# *Tagliatelle with Mushroom Sauce*

**SERVES 4 TO 6**

**TIP**

Use any sweet wine instead of Madeira.

Substitute the white part of one green onion for the shallot.

| | | |
|---|---|---|
| 1 lb | tagliatelle or fettuccine | 500 g |
| 3 tbsp | butter | 45 mL |
| 1 | shallot, chopped | 1 |
| 8 oz | mushrooms (preferably wild), sliced | 250 g |
| 1/4 cup | Madeira or port | 50 mL |
| 1/3 cup | chicken stock | 75 mL |
| 1 1/2 cups | whipping (35%) cream | 375 mL |
| | Salt and pepper to taste | |

1. In a large pot of boiling salted water, cook tagliatelle 8 to 10 minutes or until *al dente*. Meanwhile, prepare the sauce.

2. In a large saucepan, melt butter over medium–high heat. Add shallot and mushrooms; cook until tender. Remove from pan and set aside. Add Madeira to pan, increase heat and cook until almost evaporated. Add chicken stock, reduce heat to medium and cook 1 minute. Add cream; cook 3 minutes longer. Stir in mushrooms; season to taste with salt and pepper.

3. Toss drained pasta with sauce. Serve immediately.

*— Daniel's —*
*Tuscon*

# Spaghettini with Sun-Dried Tomatoes and Broccoli

**SERVES 4 TO 6**

**TIP**

To toast pine nuts, bake in 350° F (180° C) oven about 8 minutes or until golden and fragrant.

It's more economical to buy dry-packed sun-dried tomatoes and rehydrate them yourself than to buy oil-packed. To rehydrate, bring a pan of water to a boil, add sun-dried tomatoes, reduce heat and simmer 5 minutes. Drain and use immediately, or put in a jar, add olive oil to cover, and refrigerate for later use.

| | | |
|---|---|---|
| 12 oz | spaghettini | 375 g |
| 2 cups | broccoli florets | 500 mL |
| 1/2 cup | olive oil | 125 mL |
| 2 tbsp | minced garlic | 25 mL |
| Pinch | hot pepper flakes | Pinch |
| 3/4 cup | chopped, drained, sun-dried tomatoes, packed in oil | 175 mL |
| 1/2 cup | chopped fresh basil (or 2 tsp [10 mL] dried) | 125 mL |
| 1/2 cup | grated Parmesan cheese | 125 mL |
| 1/3 cup | toasted pine nuts | 75 mL |

1. In a large pot of boiling salted water, cook spaghettini 8 to 10 minutes or until *al dente*. Meanwhile, prepare the sauce.
2. In a pot of boiling water, blanch broccoli 2 minutes; refresh in cold water and drain. Set aside.
3. In a large skillet, heat oil over medium-high heat. Add garlic and hot pepper flakes; cook, stirring, 1 minute. Add broccoli and sun-dried tomatoes; cook 1 minute longer.
4. Toss drained pasta with broccoli mixture, basil and Parmesan. Serve immediately, garnished with pine nuts.

— *Scoozi* —
*Chicago*

# *Fettuccine with Artichokes and Mushroom Sauce*

**SERVES 4 TO 6**

**TIP**

Use canned drained artichoke hearts, or cook your own. To cook artichoke hearts: trim the leaves and choke from 10 artichokes, in a saucepan melt 2 tsp (10 mL) butter over medium heat, and saute artichoke hearts until tender when pierced with the tip of a knife.

| | | |
|---|---|---|
| 10 | artichoke hearts (fresh cooked or canned, drained) | 10 |
| 1/4 cup | vegetable oil | 50 mL |
| 1/2 lb | mushrooms, chopped | 250 g |
| 1/2 tsp | minced garlic | 2 mL |
| 1/4 cup | dry white wine | 50 mL |
| 1 1/2 cups | whipping (35%) cream | 375 mL |
| 1/2 tsp | ground saffron | 2 mL |
| 1 lb | fettuccine | 500 g |
| 1/3 cup | grated Parmesan cheese | 75 mL |
| | Salt and pepper to taste | |
| | Fresh parsley sprigs | |

1. Chop 6 of the artichoke hearts; set aside.
2. In a large skillet, heat oil over medium–high heat. Add mushrooms and garlic; cook 5 minutes. Add chopped artichokes and wine; cook 2 minutes. Stir in cream; bring to a boil. Stir in saffron, reduce heat to low and simmer 5 minutes.
3. Meanwhile, in a large pot of boiling salted water, cook fettuccine 8 to 10 minutes or until *al dente*; drain.
4. Toss pasta with artichoke sauce and Parmesan. Season to taste with salt and pepper. Serve immediately, garnished with whole artichoke hearts and parsley.

— *La Sila* —
*Montreal*

# Linguine with Yellow Pepper Sauce

SERVES 4 TO 6

TIP

For a special dinner, use black squid pasta — the color contrast is beautiful!

| | | |
|---|---|---:|
| 1 lb | linguine or fettuccine | 500 g |
| 1/2 cup | butter | 125 mL |
| 2 | yellow peppers, cut in strips | 2 |
| 2 | cloves garlic, crushed | 2 |
| 1 | shallot or green onion, chopped | 1 |
| 1 | bay leaf | 1 |
| 1/2 cup | chicken stock | 125 mL |
| | Salt and pepper to taste | |

1. In a large pot of boiling salted water, cook linguine 8 to 10 minutes or until *al dente*. Meanwhile, prepare the sauce.

2. In a large skillet, melt 1/4 cup (50 mL) of the butter over medium-high heat. Add pepper strips, garlic and shallot; cook, stirring, until peppers are softened. Stir in bay leaf and chicken stock; cook 5 minutes. Remove bay leaf. In food processor, purée sauce with remaining butter. Season to taste with salt and pepper.

3. Toss drained pasta with sauce. Serve immediately.

*— Monte Carlo Living Room —*

*Philadelphia*

# Penne with Mushrooms in a Light Cream Sauce

**SERVES 4 TO 6**

**TIP**

Use a combination of mushrooms — common, oyster, porcini, chanterelle, etc.

| | | |
|---|---|---|
| 3 tbsp | butter | 45 mL |
| 1 tbsp | minced shallots or onions | 15 mL |
| 3 cups | chopped mushrooms | 750 mL |
| 1 1/2 cups | whipping (35%) cream | 375 mL |
| 1 lb | penne | 500 g |
| 1/4 cup | grated Parmesan cheese | 50 mL |
| Pinch | chopped fresh parsley | Pinch |
| | Pepper to taste | |

1. In a large skillet, melt butter over medium-high heat. Add shallots and cook, stirring, 1 minute. Stir in mushrooms; cook 5 minutes or until mushrooms brown. Stir in cream; cook until sauce thickens, about 5 minutes.

2. Meanwhile, in a large pot of boiling salted water, cook penne 8 to 10 minutes or until *al dente*; drain.

3. Toss pasta with sauce, Parmesan and parsley. Season to taste with pepper. Serve immediately.

*— Biffi Bistro —*
*Toronto*

# Rigatoni with Artichokes

**SERVES 4 TO 5**

**TIP**

If prosciutto is unavailable, use ham. Omit artichokes and increase peas to 1 cup (250 mL), if desired.

Use canned drained artichoke hearts, or cook your own. To cook artichoke hearts: trim the leaves and choke from 2 artichokes, in a saucepan melt 2 tsp (10 mL) butter over medium heat, and saute sliced artichoke hearts until tender when pierced with the tip of a knife.

| | | |
|---|---|---|
| 12 oz | rigatoni | 375 g |
| 2 | cooked artichoke hearts, sliced | 2 |
| 2 tbsp | butter | 25 mL |
| 1/2 cup | chopped onions | 125 mL |
| 3 oz | prosciutto, chopped | 75 g |
| 1/2 cup | finely diced carrots | 125 mL |
| 1/2 cup | white wine | 125 mL |
| 2/3 cup | peas, fresh or frozen | 150 mL |
| 1/4 cup | chicken stock | 50 mL |
| 1 cup | whipping (35%) cream | 250 mL |
| | Salt and pepper to taste | |

1. In a large pot of boiling salted water cook rigatoni 8 to 10 minutes or until *al dente*. Meanwhile, prepare the sauce.

2. In a large skillet, melt butter over medium-high heat. Add onions and cook until soft. Stir in artichokes, prosciutto and carrots; cook until carrots are softened. Stir in white wine; cook until almost all the liquid has evaporated, about 2 minutes. Stir in peas and chicken stock; bring to a boil. Stir in cream; cook 2 minutes longer. Season to taste with salt and pepper.

3. Toss drained pasta with sauce. Serve immediately.

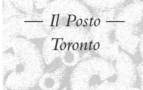

— *Il Posto* —
*Toronto*

# *Rigatoni with Eggplant and Puréed Tomatoes*

**SERVES 4 TO 6**

| | | |
|---|---|---:|
| 1/3 cup | olive oil | 75 mL |
| 12 oz | eggplant, diced | 375 g |
| 1 | can (28 oz [796 mL]) tomatoes, with juice | 1 |
| 12 oz | rigatoni | 375 g |
| | Salt and pepper to taste | |
| 2 tbsp | chopped fresh basil (or 1 1/2 tsp [7 mL] dried) | 25 mL |
| 1/2 cup | grated Parmesan cheese | 125 mL |

1. In a large saucepan, heat olive oil over medium-high heat. Add eggplant and cook until golden, about 5 minutes, adding more olive oil if necessary. Meanwhile, in food processor purée tomatoes. Add puréed tomatoes and dried basil, if using, to eggplant; bring to a boil, reduce heat to simmer and cook 15 to 20 minutes, or until thickened.

2. Meanwhile, in a large pot of boiling salted water, cook rigatoni 8 to 10 minutes or until *al dente*; drain.

3. Season sauce with salt and pepper to taste. Stir in fresh basil, if using. Toss pasta with sauce. Serve immediately, sprinkled with Parmesan.

*— Cafe Trevi —*
*New York*

# Pasta with Spinach Pesto

**TIP**

Substitute chopped walnuts
for the pine nuts.

| | | |
|---|---|---|
| 1 lb | fresh spinach, washed and stemmed | 500 g |
| 8 oz | fettuccine | 250 g |
| 1/3 cup | olive oil | 75 mL |
| 1/3 cup | pine nuts | 75 mL |
| 1 1/2 tsp | chopped garlic | 7 mL |
| 1/3 cup | grated Parmesan cheese | 75 mL |
| | Salt and pepper to taste | |

1. In a saucepan bring 1 cup (250 mL) water to a boil. Add spinach; cook just until spinach wilts. Drain spinach, squeeze out moisture and chop finely. Set aside.
2. In a large pot of boiling salted water, cook fettuccine 8 to 10 minutes or until *al dente*. Meanwhile, prepare the sauce.
3. In a large skillet, heat oil over medium-high heat. Add pine nuts and cook until golden. Stir in spinach and garlic; reduce heat to low and cook 3 minutes.
4. Toss drained pasta with sauce and Parmesan cheese. Season to taste with salt and pepper. Serve immediately.

*Cafe des Artistes*
*New York*

# Bow Ties in Mushroom Tomato Sauce

**SERVES 4 TO 5**

**TIP**

Use a combination of different varieties of mushrooms — cultivated, oyster, porcini or chanterelles.

| | | |
|---|---|---|
| 12 oz | bow tie pasta (farfalle) | 375 g |
| 1/4 cup | butter | 50 mL |
| 3 cups | chopped mushrooms | 750 mL |
| 2 tsp | minced garlic | 10 mL |
| 2 tbsp | chopped shallots or onions | 25 mL |
| Pinch | dried rosemary | Pinch |
| 3/4 cup | prepared tomato sauce | 175 mL |
| 3/4 cup | whipping (35%) cream | 175 mL |
| 1/3 cup | grated Parmesan cheese | 75 mL |

1. In a large pot of boiling salted water, cook farfalle 8 to 10 minutes or until *al dente*. Meanwhile, prepare the sauce.

2. In a large skillet, melt butter over medium–high heat. Add mushrooms and cook until golden, about 5 minutes. Stir in garlic, shallots and rosemary; cook until shallots are softened. Stir in tomato sauce and cream; cook 3 minutes or until sauce thickens.

3. Toss drained pasta with sauce and Parmesan cheese. Serve immediately.

*Il Nido/Il Monello-*
*New York*

# *Bow Ties with Wild Mushrooms*

**SERVES 4 TO 6**

| | | |
|---|---|---|
| 1 lb | bow tie pasta (farfalle) | 500 g |
| 1/3 cup | olive oil | 75 mL |
| 12 oz | wild mushrooms, (oyster or porcini), sliced | 375 g |
| 4 | cloves garlic, crushed | 4 |
| 1/4 cup | butter | 50 mL |
| 2 cups | chicken stock | 500 mL |
| 3/4 cup | grated Parmesan cheese | 175 mL |
| 3 tbsp | chopped fresh parsley | 45 mL |
| | Salt and pepper to taste | |

1. In a large pot of boiling salted water, cook farfalle 8 to 10 minutes or until *al dente*. Meanwhile, prepare the sauce.

2. In a large skillet, heat oil over medium–high heat. Add mushrooms and garlic; cook until golden, about 5 minutes. Stir in butter and chicken stock; cook 5 minutes longer.

3. Toss drained pasta with sauce, Parmesan and parsley. Season to taste with salt and pepper. Serve immediately.

*Ristorante Primavera*
*New York*

# Penne with Mushroom and Onion Sauce

**TIP**

If using wild mushrooms, try oyster or shiitake.

| | | |
|---|---|---|
| 1/4 cup | olive oil | 50 mL |
| 3 | onions, thinly sliced | 3 |
| 1 lb | penne | 500 g |
| 1 lb | mushrooms (preferably wild), sliced | 500 g |
| 3 | cloves garlic, crushed | 3 |
| 1 tbsp | minced fresh rosemary (or 1/2 tsp [2 mL] dried) | 15 mL |
| 1/2 cup | grated Parmesan cheese | 125 mL |
| | Fresh basil leaves | |

1. In a large skillet, heat 2 tbsp (25 mL) of the olive oil over medium-high heat. Add onions and cook until tender. In food processor, purée onions; set aside.

2. In a large pot of boiling salted water, cook penne 8 to 10 minutes or until *al dente*. Meanwhile, prepare the sauce.

3. In a large saucepan, heat remaining olive oil over medium-high heat. Add mushrooms, garlic and rosemary; cook about 5 minutes or until tender. Stir in onion purée.

4. Toss drained pasta with sauce and Parmesan cheese. Serve immediately, garnished with basil.

*— Paola's —*
*New York*

# *Linguine with Chickpea Sauce*

**TIP**

Try 1/4 tsp (1 mL) hot pepper flakes to start — you can add more to taste before tossing the sauce with the pasta.

| | | |
|---|---|---|
| 3 tbsp | olive oil | 45 mL |
| 3 | cloves garlic, crushed | 3 |
| 4 | fresh sage leaves, chopped (or 1/4 tsp [1 mL] dried) | 4 |
| Pinch | fresh or dried rosemary | Pinch |
| | Hot pepper flakes to taste | |
| 2 cups | chicken stock | 500 mL |
| 2 tbsp | tomato paste | 25 mL |
| 1 1/2 cups | canned chickpeas, rinsed and drained | 375 mL |
| 12 oz | linguine | 375 g |

1.  In a large saucepan, heat oil over medium–high heat. Add garlic, sage, rosemary and hot pepper flakes; cook, stirring, 1 minute. Stir in chicken stock and tomato paste; cook 5 minutes. Stir in chickpeas; cook 10 minutes.

2.  Meanwhile, in a large pot of boiling salted water, cook linguine 8 to 10 minutes or until *al dente*; drain.

3.  In food processor, purée sauce. Toss pasta with sauce. Serve immediately.

*Toscano's Restaurant Boston*

# PASTA WITH *Meat* OR *Poultry*

# *Linguine with Spicy Sausage*

**SERVES 4 TO 5**

**TIP**

Use Italian sausage with fennel seeds for a delicious variation.

| | | |
|---|---|---|
| 12 oz | linguine | 375 g |
| 1/4 cup | olive oil | 50 mL |
| 12 oz | spicy Italian sausage, casings removed | 375 g |
| 2 tbsp | chopped fresh basil (or 2 tsp [10 mL] dried) | 25 mL |
| Pinch | hot pepper flakes, or to taste | Pinch |
| | Salt and pepper to taste | |
| 1/4 cup | grated Parmesan cheese | 50 mL |
| 1 tbsp | chopped fresh parsley | 15 mL |

1. In a large pot of boiling salted water, cook linguine 8 to 10 minutes or until *al dente*. Meanwhile, prepare the sauce.

2. In a large skillet, heat oil over medium-high heat. Add sausage meat and cook, stirring to break up, until no longer pink, about 5 minutes. Stir in basil and hot pepper flakes; cook 2 minutes.

3. Toss drained pasta with sauce. Season to taste with salt and pepper. Serve immediately, sprinkled with Parmesan cheese and parsley.

*Umberto al Porto*
*Vancouver*

# *Macaroni with Chicken and Sun-Dried Tomatoes*

**SERVES 4 TO 6**

**TIP**

It's more economical to buy dry-packed sun-dried tomatoes and rehydrate them yourself than to buy oil-packed. To rehydrate, bring a pan of water to a boil, add sun-dried toma-toes, reduce heat and sim-mer 5 minutes. Drain and use immediately, or put in a jar, add olive oil to cover, and refrigerate for later use.

| | | |
|---|---|---|
| 12 oz | elbow macaroni | 375 g |
| 1 1/4 cups | whipping (35%) cream | 300 mL |
| 1 cup | diced, cooked chicken (preferably roasted or smoked) | 250 mL |
| 3 tbsp | chopped, drained, sun-dried tomatoes, packed in oil | 45 mL |
| 2 tsp | minced garlic | 10 mL |
| 1/4 cup | butter | 50 mL |
| 1/4 cup | grated Parmesan cheese | 50 mL |
| Pinch | nutmeg | Pinch |
| | Salt and pepper to taste | |

1. In a large pot of boiling salted water, cook macaroni 8 to 10 minutes or until *al dente*. Meanwhile, prepare the sauce.

2. In a large saucepan, combine cream, chicken, sun-dried tomatoes and garlic. Bring to a boil, reduce heat to low and cook 5 minutes. Stir in butter, Parmesan and nutmeg. Remove from heat. Season to taste with salt and pepper.

3. Toss drained pasta with sauce. Serve immediately.

— *The Donatello* —
*San Francisco*

# Linguine with Italian Sausage and Red Wine Sauce

**SERVES 4 TO 6**

**TIP**

Use a mild sweet Italian sausage for a less spicy dish; use a hot Italian sausage if you like a lot of spice.

| | | |
|---|---|---|
| 2 tbsp | butter | 25 mL |
| 1 tbsp | olive oil | 15 mL |
| 1 cup | chopped onions | 250 mL |
| 12 oz | medium spicy Italian sausage, casings removed | 375 g |
| 2 cups | prepared tomato sauce | 500 mL |
| 3/4 cup | red wine | 175 mL |
| 2 tbsp | butter | 25 mL |
| 12 oz | linguine | 375 g |
| | Salt and pepper to taste | |
| 1/4 cup | grated Parmesan cheese | 50 mL |

1. In a large skillet, heat butter and oil over medium-high heat. Add onions and cook until softened. Add sausage meat and cook, stirring to break up, until no longer pink, about 5 minutes. Stir in tomato sauce, red wine and butter; cook over low heat until thick, about 10 minutes.

2. Meanwhile, in a large pot of boiling salted water, cook linguine 8 to 10 minutes or until *al dente*; drain.

3. Toss pasta with sauce. Season to taste with salt and pepper. Serve immediately, sprinkled with Parmesan.

*— Il Fornaio —*
*San Francisco*

# *Fettuccine with Pancetta and Fresh Vegetables*

**SERVES 4 TO 6**

**TIP**

Use bacon if pancetta is unavailable.

| | | |
|---|---|---|
| 12 oz | fettuccine | 375 g |
| 2 tbsp | olive oil | 25 mL |
| 4 oz | chopped pancetta | 125 g |
| 2/3 cup | chopped broccoli | 150 mL |
| 2/3 cup | chopped mushrooms | 150 mL |
| 2/3 cup | chopped tomatoes | 150 mL |
| 1/3 cup | finely chopped carrots | 75 mL |
| 1 cup | whipping (35%) cream | 250 mL |
| 1/4 cup | grated Parmesan cheese | 50 mL |
| 1 tbsp | butter | 15 mL |
| | Salt and pepper to taste | |

1. In a large pot of boiling salted water, cook fettuccine 8 to 10 minutes or until *al dente*. Meanwhile, prepare the sauce.

2. In a large skillet, heat oil over medium–high heat. Add pancetta and cook until crispy, about 5 minutes. Stir in broccoli, mushrooms, tomatoes and carrots; cook 5 minutes. Stir in cream, Parmesan and butter; cook 2 minutes longer.

3. Toss drained pasta with sauce. Season to taste with salt and pepper. Serve immediately.

*On Broadway Ristorante*

*Fort Worth*

# Peppers Stuffed with Capellini and Prosciutto

**SERVES 6**

**TIP**

Remove pepper skins under cool running water.

Use ham if prosciutto is unavailable.

You can omit the peppers and serve the pasta on its own, sprinkled with grated Parmesan or Romano cheese.

— Daniel's —
Tuscon

**Preheat broiler**

| | | |
|---|---|---|
| 6 | red or yellow peppers | 6 |
| 12 oz | capellini | 375 g |
| 1 tbsp | olive oil | 15 mL |
| 1 tsp | minced garlic | 5 mL |
| 1 1/4 cups | chicken stock | 300 mL |
| 1 | large tomato, chopped | 1 |
| 1/4 cup | butter | 50 mL |
| 1 tbsp | chopped fresh basil (or 1 tsp [5 mL] dried) | 15 mL |
| 4 | slices prosciutto, cut into strips | 4 |
| | pepper to taste | |

1. Broil peppers in oven, turning often, for 15 minutes or until charred. Cool. With a sharp knife, slice off tops of peppers and set aside; peel skin and remove seeds, leaving whole pepper intact.
2. In a large pot of boiling salted water, cook capellini 6 to 8 minutes or until *al dente*. Meanwhile, prepare the sauce.
3. In a large skillet, heat oil over medium-high heat. Add garlic and cook until golden. Stir in chicken stock and tomato; cook 3 minutes. Reduce heat to medium-low. Stir in butter and basil; mix well.
4. Toss drained pasta with sauce and prosciutto. Season to taste with pepper. Stuff peppers; replace pepper tops and serve.

# *Spaghetti with Chicken Livers*

**SERVES 4 TO 5**

| | | |
|---|---|---|
| 3 tbsp | oil | 45 mL |
| 2 tbsp | butter | 25 mL |
| 1/2 cup | chopped onions | 125 mL |
| 6 | chicken livers, trimmed and chopped | 6 |
| 1 3/4 cups | canned tomatoes and juice, crushed | 425 mL |
| 1 tbsp | chopped fresh basil (or 1/2 tsp [2 mL] dried) | 15 mL |
| 12 oz | spaghetti | 375 g |
| 1/4 cup | grated Parmesan cheese | 50 mL |
| | Salt and pepper to taste | |

1. In a large skillet, heat oil and butter over medium heat. Add onions and cook until golden. Stir in chicken livers; cook 1 minute, stirring. Stir in tomatoes and basil; cook 15 minutes, stirring often.
2. Meanwhile, in a large pot of boiling salted water, cook spaghetti 8 to 10 minutes or until *al dente*; drain.
3. Toss pasta with sauce and Parmesan. Season to taste with salt and pepper. Serve immediately.

*— La Riviera —*
*New Orleans*

# *Shell Pasta with Sweet Sausage*

**SERVES 2 TO 4**

**TIP**

Substitute whole milk for the half-and-half cream, if desired.

| | | |
|---|---|---|
| 8 oz | small shell pasta | 250 g |
| 1 tbsp | olive oil | 15 mL |
| 6 oz | sweet Italian sausage, casings removed | 175 g |
| 1/2 cup | whipping (35%) cream | 125 mL |
| 1/2 cup | half-and-half (10%) cream | 125 mL |
| 1/3 cup | grated Parmesan cheese | 75 mL |
| 1 tbsp | fresh chopped parsley | 15 mL |
| Pinch | nutmeg | Pinch |
| Pinch | pepper | Pinch |

1. In a large pot of boiling salted water, cook shell pasta 8 to 10 minutes or until *al dente*. Meanwhile, prepare the sauce.
2. In a skillet heat oil over medium-high heat. Add sausage meat and cook, stirring to break up, until no longer pink, about 5 minutes. Remove from heat.
3. In a saucepan, bring whipping cream and half-and-half cream to a boil. Stir in cooked sausage, Parmesan, parsley, nutmeg and pepper; cook until heated through.
4. Toss drained pasta with sauce. Serve immediately.

*— Avanzare —*
*Chicago*

# Fusilli with Sausage and Mushrooms

**SERVES 6 TO 8
AS AN APPETIZER**

**TIP**

Use mild, medium or spicy Italian sausage, according to your taste.

| | | |
|---|---|---|
| 1/3 cup | olive oil | 75 mL |
| 12 oz | Italian sausage, casings removed | 375 g |
| 1 cup | chopped onions | 250 mL |
| 4 oz | mushrooms, chopped | 125 g |
| 1/2 cup | prepared tomato sauce | 125 mL |
| 1/4 cup | dry white wine | 50 mL |
| 1 tbsp | butter | 15 mL |
| 1 tsp | chopped fresh parsley | 5 mL |
| 1 1/2 cups | whipping (35%) cream | 375 mL |
| 1 lb | fusilli | 500 g |
| 3/4 cup | grated Parmesan cheese | 175 mL |

1. In a skillet heat 3 tbsp (45 mL) of the oil over medium-high heat. Add sausage meat and cook, stirring to break up, until no longer pink, about 5 minutes. Set aside.

2. In a large saucepan, heat remaining oil over medium-high heat. Add onions and cook until golden. Stir in mushrooms; cook until softened. Stir in sausage meat; cook 2 minutes. Stir in tomato sauce, wine, butter and parsley; mix well. Stir in cream; cook over low heat 20 to 30 minutes, stirring frequently, or until thickened.

3. Meanwhile, in large pot of boiling salted water, cook fusilli 8 to 10 minutes or until *al dente*; drain.

4. Toss pasta with sauce and Parmesan cheese. Serve immediately.

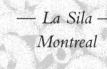

*— La Sila —*
*Montreal*

# Spaghetti with Sausage and Tomatoes

**SERVES 4 TO 6**

| | | |
|---|---|---|
| 1/4 cup | olive oil | 50 mL |
| 1 cup | finely chopped onions | 250 mL |
| 6 oz | medium spicy sausage, casings removed | 175 g |
| 1/2 cup | red wine | 125 mL |
| 3 | small tomatoes, chopped | 3 |
| 1 tbsp | chopped fresh basil (or 1/2 tsp [2 mL] dried) | 15 mL |
| Pinch | cayenne pepper | Pinch |
| 12 oz | spaghetti | 375 g |
| 1/4 cup | grated Parmesan cheese | 50 mL |
| | Salt to taste | |

1. In a large saucepan, heat olive oil over medium heat. Add onions and cook until softened. Add sausage meat and cook, stirring to break up, until no longer pink, about 5 minutes. Stir in red wine, tomatoes, basil and cayenne pepper; cook,stirring often, until sauce thickens, about 10 minutes.

2. Meanwhile, in a large pot of boiling salted water, cook spaghetti 8 to 10 minutes or until *al dente*; drain.

3. Toss pasta with sauce and Parmesan. Season to taste with salt. Serve immediately.

— *Da Marcello* —
*Montreal*

# Fettuccine with Cheese, Tomatoes and Italian Sausage

**SERVES 2 TO 4**

| | | |
|---|---|---|
| 6 oz | medium spicy Italian sausage, casings removed | 175 g |
| 8 oz | fettuccine | 250 g |
| 2 tbsp | butter | 25 mL |
| 1 tsp | minced garlic | 5 mL |
| 1 1/2 cups | canned plum tomatoes and juice, chopped | 375 mL |
| 1/3 cup | white wine | 75 mL |
| 2 tbsp | chopped fresh basil (or 1 1/2 tsp [7 mL] dried) | 25 mL |
| 1 tbsp | grated Parmesan or Romano cheese | 15 mL |
| | Salt and pepper to taste | |
| 4 oz | mozzarella, finely diced | 125 g |

1. In a skillet over medium–high heat, cook sausage meat, stirring to break up, until no longer pink, about 5 minutes. Set aside.

2. In a large pot of boiling water, cook fettuccine 8 to 10 minutes or until *al dente*. Meanwhile, prepare the sauce.

3. In a large saucepan, melt butter over medium–high heat. Add garlic and cook until golden. Stir in tomatoes, wine and basil; cook 5 minutes. Stir in sausage and Parmesan cheese; cook until heated through.

4. Toss drained pasta with sauce. Season to taste with salt and pepper. Stir in mozzarella. Serve immediately.

*The Brass Elephant*
*Baltimore*

# Linguine with Chicken, Mushrooms and Sun-Dried Tomatoes

**TIP**

Use oyster or shiitake mushrooms for a deep mushroomy flavor.

It's more economical to buy dry-packed sun-dried tomatoes and rehydrate them yourself than to buy oil-packed. To rehydrate, bring a pan of water to a boil, add sun-dried tomatoes, reduce heat and simmer 5 minutes. Drain and use immediately, or put in a jar, add olive oil to cover, and refrigerate for later use.

| | | |
|---|---|---|
| 12 oz | linguine, preferably whole wheat | 375 g |
| 3 tbsp | olive oil | 45 mL |
| 2 tsp | minced garlic | 10 mL |
| 12 oz | chicken breast, cubed | 375 g |
| | Flour for dusting chicken | |
| 2 cups | chicken stock | 500 mL |
| 1/4 cup | white wine | 50 mL |
| 2 tbsp | chopped green onions | 25 mL |
| 2 tbsp | chopped, drained sun-dried tomatoes, packed in oil | 25 mL |
| 8 oz | mushrooms (preferably wild), chopped | 250 g |

1.  In a large pot of boiling salted water, cook linguine 8 to 10 minutes or until *al dente*. Meanwhile, prepare the sauce.

2.  In a large saucepan, heat oil over medium-high heat. Add garlic and cook until golden. Dust chicken with flour; add to pan and cook, stirring, until browned. Stir in chicken stock, wine, green onions, sun-dried tomatoes and mushrooms; cook 5 minutes.

3.  Toss drained pasta with sauce. Serve immediately.

*— Dalesio's —*
*Baltimore*

# Linguine with Lychees, Chicken and Cashews

**SERVES 4 TO 6**

**TIP**

Lychees are a Chinese fruit available in cans in the Chinese section of the supermarket.

| | | |
|---|---|---|
| 1 lb | linguine | 500 g |
| 2 tbsp | butter | 25 mL |
| 8 oz | cooked chicken, diced (preferably smoked or roasted) | 250 g |
| 1 | can (4 oz [125 mL]) lychees, drained and chopped | 1 |
| 1 cup | whipping (35%) cream | 250 mL |
| 1 cup | prepared tomato sauce | 250 mL |
| 1/3 cup | chopped cashews | 75 mL |
| 1/3 cup | chopped green onions | 75 mL |
| 1/4 cup | grated Parmesan cheese | 50 mL |
| | Pepper to taste | |

1. In a large pot of boiling salted water, cook linguine 8 to 10 minutes or until *al dente*. Meanwhile, prepare the sauce.

2. In a large skillet, melt butter over medium-high heat. Add chicken and lychees; cook until chicken starts to brown, about 4 minutes. Stir in cream and tomato sauce; cook 5 minutes.

3. Toss drained pasta with sauce, cashews and green onions. Serve immediately, sprinkled with Parmesan and pepper.

— *Biffi Bistro* —
*Toronto*

# Fettuccine with Beef Tenderloin and Chicken

**SERVES 4 TO 6**

**TIP**

*Gari,* the pickled ginger served with sushi, is available in the specialty section of the supermarket.

| | | |
|---|---|---|
| 2 tbsp | olive oil | 25 mL |
| 6 oz | thinly sliced beef tenderloin | 175 g |
| 6 oz | thinly sliced chicken breast | 175 g |
| 1/4 cup | finely chopped *gari* (pickled ginger) | 50 mL |
| 1 lb | fettuccine | 500 g |
| 2 tbsp | chopped fresh basil (or 1/2 tsp [2 mL] dried) | 25 mL |
| 1 tsp | minced garlic | 5 mL |
| 1 1/2 cups | whipping (35%) cream | 375 mL |
| 1/4 cup | grated Parmesan cheese | 50 mL |
| | Pepper to taste | |

1. In a large skillet, heat oil over medium–high heat. Add beef, chicken and ginger; cook, stirring, just until meat is cooked through. Remove from heat; remove meat from skillet and set aside.

2. In a large pot of boiling salted water, cook fettuccine 8 to 10 minutes or until *al dente.* Meanwhile, prepare the sauce.

3. Heat same skillet (as in Step 1) over medium–high heat. Add basil and garlic; cook until golden. Stir in cream; reduce heat and cook until thickened, about 5 minutes.

4. Toss drained pasta with sauce. Serve immediately, sprinkled with Parmesan and pepper.

— *Biffi Bistro* —
*Toronto*

PEPPERS STUFFED WITH CAPELLINI AND PROSCIUTTO (PAGE 56) ➤

*OVERLEAF:* FETTUCCINE WITH CALAMARI IN A SPICY MEDITERRANEAN SAUCE (PAGE 96) ➤

# *Bow Tie Pasta with Chicken and Green Olives*

**SERVES 4 TO 5**

**TIP**

Use bacon if pancetta is unavailable.

Try duck instead of chicken — it works especially well with this spicy sauce.

| | | |
|---|---|---|
| 12 oz | bow tie pasta (farfalle) | 375 g |
| 3 oz | pancetta, diced | 75 g |
| 3 oz | spicy sausage, casings removed | 75 g |
| 2 tbsp | chopped fresh rosemary (or 1/2 tsp [2 mL] dried) | 25 mL |
| 2 tbsp | chopped fresh sage (or 1/2 tsp [2 mL] dried) | 25 mL |
| 3 | cloves garlic, minced | 3 |
| 15 | green olives, pitted | 15 |
| Pinch | hot pepper flakes | Pinch |
| 1 1/2 cups | chicken stock | 375 mL |
| 1 tbsp | lemon juice | 15 mL |
| 1 tbsp | cornstarch | 15 mL |
| 6 oz | cooked chicken, thinly sliced | 175 g |
| | Salt and pepper to taste | |

1. In a large pot of boiling salted water, cook bow tie pasta 8 to 10 minutes or until *al dente*. Meanwhile, prepare the sauce.

2. In a large skillet, cook pancetta and sausage meat over medium-high heat, stirring to break up, until sausage is no longer pink, about 5 minutes. Stir in rosemary, sage, garlic, olives and hot pepper flakes; cook 2 minutes, stirring. Stir in chicken stock and lemon juice; cook 5 minutes. Dissolve cornstarch in 1 tbsp (15 mL) cold water; stir into sauce and cook until thickened, about 2 minutes. Stir in chicken; cook until heated through. Season to taste with salt and pepper.

3. Toss drained pasta with sauce. Serve immediately.

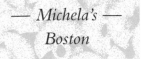

*— Michela's —*
*Boston*

< BOW TIE PASTA WITH CHICKEN AND GREEN OLIVES (THIS PAGE)

# Penne with Mushrooms and Chicken

**SERVES 4 TO 5 AS AN APPETIZER**

**TIP**

Try substituting duck for the chicken.

| | | |
|---|---|---:|
| 2 tbsp | butter | 25 mL |
| 2 tbsp | olive oil | 25 mL |
| 2 | cloves garlic, crushed | 2 |
| 1 cup | chopped onions | 250 mL |
| 1 tbsp | chopped fresh basil (or 1/2 tsp [2 mL] dried) | 15 mL |
| 1 tbsp | chopped fresh parsley (or 1 tsp [5 mL] dried) | 15 mL |
| 1/4 cup | white wine | 50 mL |
| 1/4 cup | chicken stock | 50 mL |
| 1/2 cup | whipping (35%) cream | 125 mL |
| 8 oz | penne | 250 g |
| 2 tbsp | butter | 25 mL |
| 2 tbsp | olive oil | 25 mL |
| 4 oz | cooked chicken (preferably smoked), sliced | 125 g |
| 4 oz | mushrooms (preferably a variety), chopped | 125 g |
| 1 | tomato, chopped | 1 |
| 1 | small bunch arugula, chopped | 1 |
| 1/3 cup | grated Parmesan cheese | 75 mL |

1. In a large skillet, heat butter and oil over medium heat. Add garlic, onion, basil and parsley; cook until onions are softened. Stir in wine; cook 2 minutes. Stir in chicken stock; cook 2 minutes. Stir in cream; cook 5 minutes. Set sauce aside.

2. In a large pot of boiling water, cook penne 8 to 10 minutes or until *al dente*. Meanwhile, prepare the sauce.

3. In another large skillet, heat butter and oil over medium heat. Cook chicken, mushrooms, tomato and arugula 3 minutes. Stir in cream sauce; reduce heat to low and cook 5 minutes.

4. Toss drained pasta with sauce. Serve immediately, sprinkled with Parmesan.

— *Centro* —

*Toronto*

# Spaghetti with Chicken and Broccoli

**SERVES 4 TO 6**

| | | |
|---|---|---:|
| 1 | bunch broccoli, divided into florets | 1 |
| 4 tsp | olive oil | 20 mL |
| 12 oz | chicken breast, diced | 375 g |
| 2 | plum tomatoes, diced | 2 |
| 2 tsp | minced garlic | 10 mL |
| 2/3 cup | chicken stock | 150 mL |
| 12 oz | spaghetti | 375 g |
| 1 tbsp | butter | 15 mL |
| | Salt and pepper to taste | |

1. In a large pot of boiling water, blanch broccoli for 2 minutes; refresh under cold water and drain. Set aside.

2. In a large skillet, heat oil over medium-high heat. Add chicken, tomatoes, garlic and broccoli; sauté until chicken is barely cooked, about 5 to 8 minutes. Stir in chicken stock and cook until sauce thickens, about 3 minutes.

3. Meanwhile, in a large pot of boiling salted water, cook spaghetti 8 to 10 minutes or until *al dente*; drain.

4. Toss pasta with sauce and butter. Season to taste with salt and pepper. Serve immediately.

*Upstairs at the Pudding*

*Boston*

# Fettuccine with Venison Bolognese

**SERVES 4 TO 6**

**TIP**

The venison in this recipe provides a hearty, gamy flavor. If you can't find venison, omit and use double the quantity of ground beef.

| | | |
|---|---|---|
| 1/4 cup | olive oil | 50 mL |
| 2 tbsp | butter | 25 mL |
| 4 | cloves garlic, crushed | 4 |
| 3 tbsp | finely chopped carrots | 45 mL |
| 3 tbsp | finely chopped celery | 45 mL |
| 3 tbsp | finely chopped onions | 45 mL |
| 8 oz | ground venison | 250 g |
| 8 oz | ground beef | 250 g |
| 1/2 cup | red wine | 125 mL |
| 1/2 cup | white wine | 125 mL |
| 1/2 cup | half-and-half (10%) cream | 125 mL |
| Pinch | ground nutmeg | Pinch |
| 1 | can (28 oz [796 mL]) tomatoes, drained | 1 |
| | Salt and pepper to taste | |
| 1 lb | fettuccine or tagliatelle | 500 g |
| 1/4 cup | grated Parmesan cheese | 50 mL |

1.  In a large saucepan, heat oil and butter over medium heat. Add garlic and cook 1 minute. Stir in carrots, celery and onions; cook until vegetables are softened. Add venison and beef; cook, stirring to break up, until no longer pink. Increase heat to high; stir in red and white wine and cook 3 minutes. Stir in cream and nutmeg; cook 3 minutes. Add tomatoes, stirring to break up; reduce heat to low and cook 1 1/2 hours.
2.  In a large pot of boiling salted water, cook fettuccine 8 to 10 minutes or until *al dente*; drain.
3.  Toss pasta with sauce. Season to taste with salt and pepper. Serve immediately, sprinkled with Parmesan.

*Upstairs at the Pudding*

*Boston*

# Tagliatelle Carbonara

SERVES 4 TO 5

**TIP**

Use bacon if pancetta is unavailable.

| | | |
|---|---|---|
| 6 | eggs | 6 |
| 1/3 cup | grated Parmesan cheese | 75 mL |
| 1/4 cup | whipping (35%) cream | 50 mL |
| 2 tbsp | chopped fresh parsley (or 1 tbsp [15 mL] dried) | 25 mL |
| 12 oz | tagliatelle or fettuccine | 375 g |
| 2 tbsp | butter | 25 mL |
| 1 cup | chopped onions | 250 mL |
| 1/2 cup | diced pancetta | 125 mL |

1. In a bowl, whisk together eggs, Parmesan, whipping cream and parsley; set aside.

2. In a large pot of boiling salted water, cook tagliatelle 8 to 10 minutes or until *al dente*. Meanwhile, prepare the sauce.

3. In a large saucepan, melt butter over medium heat. Add onions and pancetta; cook until onions are soft, about 5 minutes. Reduce heat to low. Add drained pasta and egg mixture to saucepan; cook, stirring, until egg has thickened, but not scrambled. Serve immediately.

*Upstairs at the Pudding*

*Boston*

# *Spaghetti with Chicken Livers and Prosciutto*

**SERVES 4 TO 6**

**TIP**

Use ham if prosciutto is unavailable.

| | | |
|---|---|---|
| 12 oz | spaghetti | 375 g |
| 3 tbsp | butter | 45 mL |
| 3 tbsp | olive oil | 45 mL |
| 12 oz | chicken livers, trimmed and halved | 375 g |
| 6 oz | prosciutto, chopped | 175 g |
| 3 tbsp | grated Parmesan cheese | 45 mL |
| 3 tbsp | butter | 45 mL |
| | Salt and pepper to taste | |

1. In a large pot of boiling salted water, cook spaghetti 8 to 10 minutes or until *al dente*. Meanwhile, prepare the sauce.

2. In a large skillet, heat butter and oil over medium-high heat. Add chicken livers and cook just until done. Stir in prosciutto, drained pasta, Parmesan and butter. Season to taste with salt and pepper. Serve immediately.

*Cafe des Artistes
New York*

# *Fettuccine with Prosciutto and Green Peas*

**SERVES 4**

**TIP**

Use ham if prosciutto is unavailable.

| | | |
|---|---|---|
| 12 oz | fettuccine | 375 g |
| 2 | eggs | 2 |
| 1/3 cup | grated Parmesan cheese | 75 mL |
| 1/2 cup | chicken stock | 125 mL |
| 1 cup | green peas, fresh or frozen | 250 mL |
| 3 tbsp | butter | 45 mL |
| 1/2 cup | chopped onions | 125 mL |
| 4 oz | prosciutto, chopped | 125 g |
| | Grated Parmesan cheese | |

1. In a large pot of boiling salted water, cook fettuccine 8 to 10 minutes or until *al dente*. Meanwhile, prepare the sauce.

2. In a bowl, whisk together eggs and Parmesan; set aside. In a small saucepan, bring chicken stock to a boil, add peas and cook until tender; set aside. In a large saucepan, melt butter over medium heat. Add onions and cook until golden. Stir in pea mixture and prosciutto; cook for 1 minute. Add drained pasta and egg mixture; toss. Serve immediately, sprinkled with extra Parmesan cheese.

*Ristorante Primavera New York*

# PASTA WITH
# *Fish* OR *Seafood*

# *Thin Pasta with Shrimp, Red Peppers and Pine Nuts*

**SERVES 2 TO 4**

**TIP**

To toast pine nuts, bake in 350° F (180° C) oven about 8 minutes or until golden and fragrant.

| | | |
|---|---|---|
| 8 oz | linguine or tagliolini | 250 g |
| 3/4 cup | white wine | 175 mL |
| 1/4 cup | chopped shallots or onions | 50 mL |
| 1/4 cup | butter | 50 mL |
| 2 tbsp | olive oil | 25 mL |
| 8 oz | medium shrimp, peeled and deveined | 250 g |
| 1 | red pepper, cut into thin strips | 1 |
| 1 | clove garlic, crushed | 1 |
| 1/3 cup | toasted pine nuts | 75 mL |
| 1 tbsp | chopped fresh basil (or 1/2 tsp [2 mL] dried) | 15 mL |
| 1 tbsp | chopped fresh oregano (or 1/2 tsp [2 mL] dried) | 15 mL |
| 1 tbsp | chopped fresh parsley | 15 mL |

1. In a large pot of boiling salted water, cook linguine 8 to 10 minutes or until *al dente*. Meanwhile, prepare the sauce.

2. In a small saucepan, bring wine and shallots to a boil; reduce heat and simmer 5 minutes. Remove from heat. Gradually whisk in butter; set aside and keep warm.

3. In a large skillet, heat oil over high heat. Add shrimp, red pepper strips, garlic and pine nuts; cook just until shrimp turns pink, about 2 minutes.

4. Toss drained pasta with shrimp mixture and wine sauce. Serve immediately, sprinkled with basil, oregano and parsley.

*Primi/Valentino*
*Los Angeles*

# Thin Pasta with Scallops

**SERVES 4**

**TIP**

Black squid pasta is available at specialty food stores.

If the fish market hasn't already done so, remove the small muscle on the side of each scallop; it toughens as it cooks.

| | | |
|---|---|---|
| 1 cup | whipping (35%) cream | 250 mL |
| 1 cup | fish stock or clam juice | 250 mL |
| 1 tbsp | cornstarch | 15 mL |
| 12 oz | linguine (preferably half regular and half black squid pasta) | 375 g |
| 1/2 tsp | ground saffron | 2 mL |
| 12 oz | bay scallops | 375 g |

1. In a saucepan bring cream and fish stock to a boil; reduce heat to low and simmer 10 minutes. Raise heat to medium. In a small bowl, dissolve cornstarch in 1/4 cup (50 mL) cold water; gradually stir into cream sauce. Cook until thickened.

2. In a large pot of boiling salted water, cook linguine 8 to 10 minutes or until *al dente*. Meanwhile, stir saffron and scallops into sauce; cook just until scallops are cooked, about 3 to 5 minutes.

3. Toss drained pasta with sauce. Serve immediately.

*Chianti Ristorante*
*Los Angeles*

# Salmon Fettuccine

**SERVES 4 TO 5**

| | | |
|---|---|---|
| 1/4 cup | butter | 50 mL |
| 1 tbsp | olive oil | 15 mL |
| 1 | carrot, thinly sliced | 1 |
| 1 | stalk celery, thinly sliced | 1 |
| 3 | cloves garlic, crushed | 3 |
| 12 oz | fettuccine | 375 g |
| 12 oz | salmon fillets, skinned, boned and cubed | 375 g |
| 1/2 cup | white wine, preferably sparkling | 125 mL |
| 1 cup | prepared tomato sauce | 250 mL |
| 1/2 cup | half-and-half (10%) cream | 125 mL |
| | Salt and pepper to taste | |

1. In a large saucepan, heat butter and oil over medium heat. Add carrot, celery and garlic; cook until very soft.

2. In a large pot of boiling salted water, cook fettuccine 8 to 10 minutes or until *al dente*. Meanwhile, add salmon to vegetables; cook over low heat 3 minutes. Stir in wine; cover and cook until sauce reduces, about 5 minutes. Stir in tomato sauce and cream; cook 2 minutes longer.

3. Toss drained pasta with sauce. Season to taste with salt and pepper. Serve immediately.

*Carlo's Restaurant*
*San Rafael*

# Linguine with Shrimp and Clams

**SERVES 4**

**TIP**

You can use mussels instead of clams.

Discard any clams or mussels that do not open.

| | | |
|---|---|---|
| 12 | medium shrimp, peeled and deveined | 12 |
| 10 | asparagus spears, cut into pieces | 10 |
| 3 tbsp | olive oil | 45 mL |
| 1 | clove garlic, crushed | 1 |
| 1 lb | fresh clams, well-scrubbed | 500 g |
| 12 oz | linguine, preferably black squid pasta | 375 g |
| 2 tbsp | olive oil | 25 mL |
| 1 | carrot, finely chopped | 1 |
| 1 | stalk celery, chopped | 1 |
| 2 | green onions, chopped | 2 |
| 3/4 cup | white wine | 175 mL |
| 1/3 cup | whipping (35%) cream | 75 mL |
| 1/3 cup | butter | 75 mL |

1. In a saucepan bring small amount of water to a boil; add shrimp and cook just until pink. Drain; cut into small pieces and set aside.

2. In a pot of boiling water, blanch asparagus pieces 1 minute; refresh in cold water and drain. Set aside.

3. In a large saucepan, heat oil over medium–high heat. Add garlic and cook until golden. Add 3/4 cup (175 mL) water; bring to a boil. Add clams, cover and cook until shells open, about 6 minutes. Remove clams from shells and set aside. Discard shells and cooking water.

4. In a large pot of boiling salted water, cook linguine 8 to 10 minutes or until *al dente*. Meanwhile, in a large skillet, heat olive oil over medium–high heat. Add carrot, celery and green onions; cook 3 minutes. Stir in wine and cream; cook 4 minutes. Stir in butter. In blender, purée mixture. Strain sauce back into skillet. Stir in shrimp, asparagus and clams; cook over medium heat just until heated through.

5. Toss drained pasta with sauce. Serve immediately.

*— The Blue Fox —*
*San Francisco*

# Fettuccine with Monkfish

**SERVES 4 TO 6**

**TIP**

If monkfish is unavailable, use any firm white fish.

If prosciutto is unavailable, use ham.

| | | |
|---|---|---:|
| 1 1/2 cups | whipping (35%) cream | 375 mL |
| 1/4 cup | chopped fresh basil (or 1 tsp [5 mL] dried) | 50 mL |
| 1 1/2 tsp | grated lemon rind | 7 mL |
| 2 tbsp | butter | 25 mL |
| 1 lb | monkfish, cut into 2-inch (5 cm) pieces | 500 g |
| 12 oz | fettuccine | 375 g |
| 3 tbsp | vodka | 45 mL |
| 2 oz | prosciutto, chopped | 50 g |
| 1/4 cup | grated Parmesan cheese | 50 mL |

1. In a saucepan heat cream, basil and lemon rind just until hot; set aside. In a large skillet, melt butter over medium heat; add monkfish and cook until just barely cooked, about 5 minutes. Remove fish, leaving pan juices in skillet, and set aside.
2. In a large pot of boiling salted water, cook fettuccine 8 to 10 minutes or until *al dente*. Meanwhile, prepare the sauce.
3. Add vodka and warmed cream mixture to pan juices in skillet. Cook over high heat 4 minutes. Add fish pieces, reduce heat to low and cook 5 minutes.
4. Toss drained pasta with sauce, prosciutto and Parmesan. Serve immediately.

— *Giuliano's* —
*Carmel*

# *Fettuccine with Scallops and Smoked Salmon*

**TIP**

If the fish market hasn't already done so, remove the small muscle on the side of each scallop; it toughens as it cooks.

For a sharper taste, use a mixture of Parmesan and Romano cheese.

Red or black lumpfish roe, available in the refrigerator section of supermarkets, is cheaper than real caviar and more readily available.

| | | |
|---|---|---|
| 12 oz | fettuccine, preferably spinach pasta | 375 g |
| 3 tbsp | butter | 45 mL |
| 1 lb | scallops | 500 g |
| 2 tbsp | minced garlic | 25 mL |
| 1 1/4 cups | whipping (35%) cream | 300 mL |
| 2 tbsp | sour cream | 25 mL |
| 1 cup | grated Parmesan cheese | 250 mL |
| 4 oz | smoked salmon, shredded | 125 g |
| | Fish roe (caviar), optional | |

1. In a large pot of boiling salted water, cook fettuccine 8 to 10 minutes or until *al dente*. Meanwhile, prepare the sauce.

2. In a large skillet, melt butter over medium-high heat. Add scallops and garlic; cook until just barely cooked, about 2 minutes. Stir in cream and sour cream; bring to a boil. Remove from heat. Stir in Parmesan cheese.

3. Toss drained pasta with sauce and smoked salmon. Serve immediately, garnished with fish roe, if desired.

*— Giuliano's —*
*Carmel*

# *Linguine with Mixed Seafood*

**SERVES 4**

**TIP**

Use the juice from the canned clams rather than bottled clam juice or fish stock.

If the fish market hasn't already done so, remove the small muscle on the side of each scallop; it toughens as it cooks.

If fresh clams are unavailable, substitute with more mussels.

| | | |
|---|---|---:|
| 12 oz | linguine | 375 g |
| 1 cup | prepared tomato sauce | 250 mL |
| 1/2 cup | clam juice or fish stock | 125 mL |
| 1/3 cup | olive oil | 75 mL |
| 1/4 cup | white wine | 50 mL |
| 10 | fresh clams | 10 |
| 10 | mussels | 10 |
| 4 oz | medium shrimp, peeled and deveined | 125 g |
| 4 oz | scallops | 125 g |
| 1/2 cup | drained canned clams | 125 mL |

1. In a large pot of boiling salted water, cook linguine 8 to 10 minutes or until *al dente*. Meanwhile, prepare the sauce.

2. In a large saucepan, bring tomato sauce, clam juice, olive oil and white wine to a boil; reduce heat to medium and cook 5 minutes. Add fresh clams, mussels, shrimp, scallops and canned clams; cover and cook just until shells open, about 5 minutes.

3. Remove shellfish from sauce. Toss sauce with drained pasta. Arrange shellfish decoratively around serving dish. Serve immediately.

*On Broadway Ristorante*

*Fort Worth*

# *Spaghetti with Escargots*

**SERVES 4 TO 6**

| | | |
|---|---|---|
| 1/4 cup | oil | 50 mL |
| 1/2 cup | chopped onions | 125 mL |
| 2 tsp | minced garlic | 10 mL |
| Pinch | cayenne pepper | Pinch |
| 1 1/2 cups | canned tomatoes and juice, crushed | 375 mL |
| 2 tbsp | chopped fresh parsley (or 1 tsp [5 mL] dried) | 25 mL |
| 12 oz | spaghetti | 375 g |
| 1 | can (4 oz [125 g]) snails, drained | 1 |
| 1/3 cup | grated Parmesan or Romano cheese | 75 mL |

1.  In a large skillet, heat oil over medium heat. Add onions, garlic and cayenne; cook until onions are softened. Stir in tomatoes and parsley; reduce heat to low and cook 10 minutes, stirring occasionally.

2.  Meanwhile, in large pot of boiling salted water, cook spaghetti 8 to 10 minutes or until *al dente*; drain. Stir snails into sauce; cook until heated through, about 3 minutes. Toss pasta with sauce. Serve immediately, sprinkled with cheese.

*Momo's Italian Specialties*

*Dallas*

# Fettuccine with Shellfish and Mushrooms

**SERVES 4 TO 6**

| | | |
|---|---|---|
| 1 lb | fettuccine | 500 g |
| 2 tbsp | oil | 25 mL |
| 1 1/2 lbs | seafood (any combination of lobster pieces, scallops or peeled and deveined shrimp) | 750 g |
| 1 tbsp | minced garlic | 15 mL |
| 1/2 cup | clam juice or fish stock | 125 mL |
| 1/4 cup | white wine | 50 mL |
| 1/2 cup | chopped tomatoes | 125 mL |
| 4 oz | mushrooms, sliced | 125 g |
| 1/2 cup | soft butter, cut into pieces | 125 mL |
| | Grated Parmesan cheese | |
| | Chopped fresh parsley | |

1. In a large pot of boiling salted water, cook fettuccine 8 to 10 minutes or until *al dente*. Meanwhile, prepare the sauce.

2. In a large saucepan, heat oil over medium-high heat. Add seafood and garlic; cook 1 minute. Stir in clam juice and wine, reduce heat to low and cook until seafood is just barely cooked, about 3 to 5 minutes. Stir in tomato and mushrooms; cook 1 minute. Gradually add butter, stirring.

3. Toss drained pasta with sauce. Serve immediately, sprinkled with Parmesan and parsley.

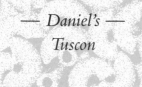

*— Daniel's —*
*Tuscon*

# Angel Hair Pasta and Smoked Salmon

**TIP**

Red or black lumpfish roe, available in the refrigerator section of supermarkets, is cheaper than real caviar and more readily available.

| | | |
|---|---|---|
| 2 tbsp | butter | 25 mL |
| 1/2 cup | chopped onions | 125 mL |
| 1 1/2 tsp | minced garlic | 7 mL |
| 5 oz | smoked salmon, shredded | 150 g |
| 1/2 cup | vodka | 125 mL |
| 3/4 cup | fish stock or clam juice | 175 mL |
| 1/2 cup | white wine | 125 mL |
| 1 1/4 cups | whipping (35%) cream | 300 mL |
| 1 lb | angel hair pasta, capellini or spaghettini | 500 g |
| | Pepper to taste | |
| 2 tsp | black fish roe (caviar), optional | 10 mL |

1. In a large skillet, melt butter over medium heat. Add onions and garlic; cook until softened. Stir in smoked salmon; cook until color changes to a pale orange, about 1 minute. Increase heat to high and stir in vodka; cook 30 seconds. With a slotted spoon, remove salmon mixture from pan, leaving liquid behind. Add fish stock and white wine to skillet; bring to a boil and cook 2 minutes. Stir in cream, reduce heat to medium and cook 5 minutes.

2. Meanwhile, in a large pot of boiling salted water, cook angel hair pasta 6 to 8 minutes or until *al dente*; drain.

3. Toss pasta with sauce. Season to taste with pepper. Serve immediately, garnished with fish roe, if desired.

*Andrea's Restaurant New Orleans*

# Fettuccine with Calamari and Eggplant

**SERVES 4**

**TIP**

Be careful not to overcook the squid or it will become rubbery.

| | | |
|---|---|---|
| 12 oz | fettuccine, preferably black squid pasta | 375 g |
| 1/3 cup | olive oil | 75 mL |
| 8 oz | eggplant, diced | 250 g |
| 2 tsp | minced garlic | 10 mL |
| 10 oz | calamari (squid), cut into 1/4-inch (5 mm) rings | 300 g |
| 1 cup | fish stock or clam juice | 250 mL |
| 1 cup | diced tomatoes | 250 mL |
| Pinch | hot pepper flakes, or to taste | Pinch |

1. In a large pot of boiling salted water, cook fettuccine 8 to 10 minutes or until *al dente*. Meanwhile, prepare the sauce.

2. In a large skillet, heat olive oil over medium-high heat. Add eggplant and garlic; cook, stirring, until golden, about 5 minutes. Stir in squid, fish stock, tomatoes and hot pepper flakes; cook until squid is just done, about 3 minutes.

3. Toss drained pasta with sauce. Serve immediately.

— *Spiaggia* —
*Chicago*

# Linguine with Shrimp and Basil Sauce

**SERVES 4**

| | | |
|---|---|---|
| 12 oz | linguine | 375 g |
| 1/3 cup | olive oil | 75 mL |
| 2 tbsp | chopped fresh basil (or 1 tsp [5 mL] dried) | 25 mL |
| 2 tsp | minced garlic | 10 mL |
| Pinch | cayenne pepper | Pinch |
| 12 oz | medium shrimp, peeled and deveined | 375 g |
| 1 1/2 cups | chopped tomatoes, preferably plum | 375 mL |
| | Salt to taste | |
| 1/4 cup | grated Parmesan cheese | 50 mL |

1.  In a large pot of boiling salted water, cook linguine 8 to 10 minutes or until *al dente*. Meanwhile, prepare the sauce.

2.  In a large skillet, heat olive oil over medium heat. Add basil, garlic and cayenne; cook, stirring, 1 minute. Stir in shrimp and tomatoes; cook just until shrimp turn pink, about 3 minutes. Season to taste with salt.

3.  Toss drained pasta with sauce. Serve immediately, sprinkled with Parmesan.

*— Avanzare —*
*Chicago*

# *Fettuccine with Mushrooms and Clams*

**SERVES 4 TO 6**

| | | |
|---|---|---|
| 3 tbsp | olive oil | 45 mL |
| 1 cup | chopped mushrooms | 250 mL |
| 1 tbsp | minced fresh parsley | 15 mL |
| 1 tsp | minced garlic | 5 mL |
| 2 | cans (each 5 oz [142 g]) clams, drained and liquid reserved | 2 |
| 1/3 cup | dry white wine | 75 mL |
| 1 1/2 cups | whipping (35%) cream | 375 mL |
| 1 lb | fettuccine | 500 g |
| 3/4 cup | grated Parmesan cheese | 175 mL |
| 1 tbsp | butter | 15 mL |
| | Salt and pepper to taste | |
| | Chopped fresh parsley | |

1. In a large skillet, heat olive oil over medium-high heat. Add mushrooms and cook until golden. Stir in parsley and garlic; cook, stirring, 2 minutes. Add clams and half their liquid to skillet (discard other half of liquid). Stir in wine; reduce heat to medium and cook 5 minutes. Stir in cream; cook 5 minutes longer.

2. Meanwhile, in large pot of boiling salted water, cook fettuccine 8 to 10 minutes or until *al dente*; drain. Stir Parmesan and butter into sauce. Toss pasta with sauce. Season to taste with salt and pepper. Serve immediately, sprinkled with chopped parsley.

— *La Sila* —
*Montreal*

# Fettuccine with Smoked Salmon and Fresh Dill

**SERVES 2 TO 4**

**TIP**

Use the white part of a green onion if shallots are unavailable.

Salmon roe is less expensive than real caviar.

| | | |
|---|---|---|
| 8 oz | fettuccine | 250 g |
| 1 tbsp | butter | 15 mL |
| 1 tbsp | chopped shallots | 15 mL |
| 4 oz | smoked salmon, shredded | 125 g |
| 1/3 cup | dry vermouth | 75 mL |
| 2 tbsp | chopped fresh dill (or 1 1/2 tsp [7 mL] dried) | 25 mL |
| 3/4 cup | whipping (35%) cream | 175 mL |
| | Pepper to taste | |
| | Dill sprigs | |
| | Salmon roe (optional) | |

1. In a large pot of boiling salted water, cook fettuccine 8 to 10 minutes or until *al dente*. Meanwhile, prepare the sauce.

2. In a large saucepan, melt butter over high heat. Add shallots and cook until softened. Stir in smoked salmon, vermouth and dill; cook 1 minute. Stir in cream; cook until slightly thickened, about 2 minutes. Season to taste with pepper.

3. Toss drained pasta with sauce. Serve immediately, garnished with dill sprigs and salmon caviar, if desired.

*The Brass Elephant*
*Baltimore*

# Fettuccine with Scallops in Tomato Sauce

**SERVES 4**

**TIP**

Delicious on any pasta, this sauce is best served over black squid pasta.

If the fish market hasn't already done so, remove the small muscle on the side of each scallop; it toughens as it cooks.

| | | |
|---|---|---|
| 3 tbsp | olive oil | 45 mL |
| 1/2 cup | chopped red onions | 125 mL |
| 1 tsp | minced garlic | 5 mL |
| 3 lb | plum tomatoes, chopped | 1.5 kg |
| 12 oz | fettuccine | 375 g |
| 1 tsp | butter | 5 mL |
| 12 | medium scallops, sliced | 12 |
| 1/3 cup | chopped fresh basil (or 1 tbsp [15 mL] dried) | 75 mL |
| | Salt and pepper to taste | |

1. In a large saucepan, heat olive oil over medium heat. Add onions and garlic; cook until softened. Stir in tomatoes; cook 15 to 20 minutes, stirring occasionally.

2. Meanwhile, in a large pot of boiling salted water, cook fettuccine 8 to 10 minutes or until *al dente*. In a small pan, melt butter over medium-high heat; add scallops and cook quickly, just until seared on both sides.

3. Stir basil into sauce; season to taste with salt and pepper. Toss drained pasta with sauce and scallops. Serve immediately.

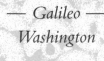

*— Galileo —*
*Washington*

# Angel Hair Pasta with Wild Mushrooms and Shrimp

**SERVES 4**

**TIP**

Use wild mushrooms—
chanterelle, oyster or
shiitake — for an extra-
special dish.

| | | |
|---|---|---|
| 8 oz | angel hair pasta, capellini or spaghettini | 250 g |
| 2 tbsp | olive oil | 25 mL |
| 6 oz | shrimp, peeled and deveined | 175 g |
| 4 oz | mushrooms, sliced | 125 g |
| 1 tsp | minced garlic | 5 mL |
| 2 tbsp | white wine | 25 mL |
| 1 cup | canned plum tomatoes and juice, crushed | 250 mL |
| 1 tbsp | chopped fresh basil (or 1 tsp [5 mL] dried) | 15 mL |
| Pinch | hot pepper flakes | Pinch |
| Pinch | dried parsley | Pinch |
| Pinch | dried thyme | Pinch |
| 3 tbsp | grated Parmesan cheese (optional) | 45 mL |
| | Pepper to taste | |
| | Fresh chopped parsley | |

1. In a large pot of boiling salted water, cook angel hair pasta 6 to 8 minutes or until *al dente*. Meanwhile, prepare the sauce.

2. In a large skillet, heat olive oil over medium-high heat. Add shrimp, mushrooms and garlic; cook just until shrimp turns pink. Stir in wine. Stir in tomatoes, basil, hot pepper flakes, parsley, thyme and Parmesan, if desired.

3. Toss drained pasta with sauce. Serve immediately, sprinkled with pepper and parsley.

*Monte Carlo
Living Room*

*Philadelphia*

# Fusilli with Tuna in a Herb Tomato Sauce

**SERVES 4 TO 6**

| | | |
|---|---|---|
| 2 tbsp | olive oil | 25 mL |
| 2 | cloves garlic, crushed | 2 |
| 4 to 6 | anchovy fillets, chopped | 4 to 6 |
| 2 tbsp | red wine | 25 mL |
| 1 | can (28 oz [796 mL]) tomatoes, undrained | 1 |
| 1 | can (6.5 oz [184 g]) tuna, drained | 1 |
| 1 lb | fusilli or rotini | 500 g |
| 2 tbsp | chopped fresh basil (or 1/2 tsp [2 mL] dried) | 15 mL |
| 1 tbsp | fresh chopped parsley | 15 mL |
| 1 tbsp | butter | 15 mL |
| 1/2 tsp | dried oregano | 2 mL |
| 1/4 tsp | dried thyme | 1 mL |
| | Pepper to taste | |
| 1/2 cup | grated Parmesan cheese | 125 mL |

1. In a large skillet, heat olive oil over medium heat. Add garlic and cook, stirring, 1 minute. Add anchovies; cook, stirring, until anchovies become paste-like. Stir in red wine, tomatoes and tuna, stirring to break up tomatoes; cook 20 minutes.

2. Meanwhile, in a large pot of boiling salted water, cook fusilli 8 to 10 minutes or until *al dente*; drain.

3. Stir basil, parsley, butter, oregano and thyme into sauce. Season to taste with pepper. Toss pasta with sauce. Serve immediately, sprinkled with Parmesan.

*— Tony's —*
*Houston*

# *Fettuccine with Smoked Salmon and Vodka*

**TIP**

Red or black lumpfish roe, available in the refrigerator section of supermarkets, is cheaper than real caviar and more readily available.

| | | |
|---|---|---|
| 2 tbsp | butter | 25 mL |
| 2 tbsp | olive oil | 25 mL |
| 1 tbsp | finely chopped onions | 15 mL |
| 1 | clove garlic, crushed | 1 |
| 4 | tomatoes, diced | 4 |
| 8 oz | smoked salmon, shredded | 250 g |
| 1 cup | whipping (35%) cream | 250 mL |
| 1/4 cup | vodka | 50 mL |
| 12 oz | fettuccine | 375 g |
| | Pepper to taste | |
| 1/4 cup | grated Parmesan cheese | 50 mL |
| 1 oz | fish roe (caviar), optional | 25 g |

1. In a large saucepan, heat butter and olive oil over medium heat. Add onions and garlic; cook 2 minutes. Stir in tomatoes; cook 5 minutes. Reduce heat to low. Stir in smoked salmon, cream and vodka; cover and cook 10 minutes, stirring occasionally.
2. Meanwhile, in a large pot of boiling salted water, cook fettuccine 8 to 10 minutes or until *al dente*; drain.
3. Toss pasta with sauce; season to taste with salt and pepper. Serve immediately, sprinkled with Parmesan and garnished with fish roe, if desired.

— *Centro* —
*Toronto*

# Linguine with Mussels, Sun-Dried Tomatoes and Olives

**TIP**

It's more economical to buy dry-packed sun-dried tomatoes and rehydrate them yourself than to buy oil-packed. To rehydrate, bring a pan of water to a boil, add sun-dried tomatoes, reduce heat and simmer 5 minutes. Drain and use immediately, or put in a jar, add olive oil to cover, and refrigerate for later use.


Discard any mussels that do not open.

| | | |
|---|---|---|
| 1 tbsp | oil | 15 mL |
| 1/4 cup | chopped onions | 50 mL |
| 1/2 cup | white wine or water | 125 mL |
| 1 lb | mussels, well-scrubbed | 500 g |
| 12 oz | linguine | 375 g |
| 2 tbsp | olive oil | 25 mL |
| 1/2 cup | chopped onions | 125 mL |
| 2 | cloves garlic, crushed | 2 |
| 4 | small tomatoes, diced | 4 |
| 1 | red pepper, cut into strips | 1 |
| 1/3 cup | chopped, drained sun-dried tomatoes packed in oil | 75 mL |
| 1/4 cup | chopped fresh basil (or 1 1/2 tsp [7 mL] dried) | 50 mL |
| 1/4 cup | sliced green olives | 50 mL |
| | Salt and pepper to taste | |

1. In a saucepan bring oil, onions and white wine to a boil. Add mussels; cover and cook just until shells open, about 3 minutes. Remove mussels from shells and set aside; strain cooking liquid and reserve.

2. In a large pot of boiling salted water, cook linguine 8 to 10 minutes or until *al dente*. Meanwhile, in a large skillet, heat olive oil over medium-high heat; add onions, garlic, tomatoes and red pepper; cook, stirring occasionally, until soft. Stir in reserved mussel liquid and mussels, sun-dried tomatoes, basil and green olives; season to taste with salt and pepper.

3. Toss drained pasta with sauce. Serve immediately.

— *Movenpick* —
*Toronto*

# Fettuccine with Mussels, Shrimp and Parsley

| | | |
|---|---|---|
| 1/2 cup | white wine | 125 mL |
| 2 | cloves garlic, crushed | 2 |
| 20 | mussels | 20 |
| 2 1/2 | slices stale white bread | 2 1/2 |
| 1/3 cup | red wine vinegar | 75 mL |
| 1 cup | well-packed fresh parsley leaves | 250 mL |
| 2 tsp | drained capers | 10 mL |
| 4 | anchovy fillets | 4 |
| 2 | cloves garlic, crushed | 2 |
| 1/3 cup | olive oil | 75 mL |
| 12 oz | fettuccine | 375 g |
| 3 oz | pancetta, chopped | 75 g |
| 12 oz | medium shrimp, peeled and deveined | 375 g |

**SERVES 4 TO 6**

**TIP**

Use bacon if pancetta is unavailable.

Flat-leaf Italian parsley is more flavorful than curly parsley.

1. In a saucepan bring wine and garlic to a boil. Add mussels; cover and cook just until shells open, about 5 minutes. Remove and discard shells; set mussels and cooking liquid aside.

2. Soak bread in vinegar 5 minutes. Drain, discarding vinegar and squeezing excess from bread. In blender or food processor, combine bread, parsley, capers, anchovies and garlic; add olive oil and purée. Set aside.

3. In a large pot of boiling salted water, cook fettuccine 8 to 10 minutes or until *al dente*. Meanwhile, in a large saucepan over medium-high heat, cook pancetta 2 minutes; stir in shrimp and cook just until pink. Add mussels and their cooking liquid; cook 1 minute longer. Stir in parsley sauce; remove from heat.

4. Toss drained pasta with sauce. Serve immediately.

— *Michela's* —
*Boston*

# *Tagliatelle with Shrimp, Garlic and Parmesan Cheese*

**SERVES 2 TO 4**

| | | |
|---|---|---|
| 8 oz | tagliatelle or fettuccine | 250 g |
| 2 tbsp | olive oil | 25 mL |
| 8 oz | shrimp, peeled and deveined | 250 g |
| 1 tbsp | minced garlic | 15 mL |
| 1/4 cup | white wine | 50 mL |
| 4 tsp | butter | 20 mL |
| 1 tbsp | olive oil | 15 mL |
| | Salt and pepper to taste | |
| 3 tbsp | grated Parmesan cheese | 45 mL |

1. In a large pot of boiling salted water, cook tagliatelle 8 to 10 minutes or until *al dente*. Meanwhile, prepare the sauce.

2. In a large skillet, heat oil over medium–high heat. Add shrimp and garlic; cook until just pink, about 3 minutes. Remove from heat. Stir in wine, butter and oil.

3. Toss drained pasta with sauce. Season to taste with salt and pepper. Serve immediately, sprinkled with Parmesan.

*— Allegro —*
*Boston*

# *Fettuccine with Scallops and Mushrooms*

**SERVES 4 TO 6**

**TIP**

Use a combination of mushrooms — cultivated and wild.

If the fish market hasn't already done so, remove the small muscle on the side of each scallop; it toughens as it cooks.

| | | |
|---|---|---:|
| 12 oz | fettuccine | 375 g |
| 2 tbsp | butter | 25 mL |
| 2 tbsp | oil | 25 mL |
| 3 cups | chopped mushrooms | 750 mL |
| 1 lb | scallops | 500 g |
| 1 1/4 cups | whipping (35%) cream | 300 mL |
| 2 tbsp | chopped fresh basil (or 1 tsp [5 mL] dried) | 25 mL |

1. In a large pot of boiling salted water, cook fettuccine 8 to 10 minutes or until *al dente*. Meanwhile, prepare the sauce.
2. In a large skillet, heat butter and oil over medium-high heat. Add mushrooms and cook until soft. Stir in scallops and cook until just barely done. Stir in cream, reduce heat to medium and cook 3 minutes. Stir in basil and remove from heat.
3. Toss drained pasta with sauce. Serve immediately.

*— Allegro —*
*Boston*

# Fettuccine with Calamari in a Spicy Mediterranean Sauce

**SERVES 4 TO 5**

**TIP**

Be careful not to overcook the squid or it will become rubbery.

| | | |
|---|---|---|
| 1/4 cup | olive oil | 50 mL |
| 3 | cloves garlic, crushed | 3 |
| 20 | black olives, pitted and chopped | 20 |
| 4 | anchovy fillets, chopped | 4 |
| 2 tbsp | drained capers | 25 mL |
| 1 | can (28 oz [796 mL]) tomatoes, with juice | 1 |
| 12 oz | fettuccine or tagliatelle | 375 g |
| 1 lb | calamari (squid), cut into 1/4-inch (5 mm) rings | 500 g |
| 1 tbsp | dried basil | 15 mL |
| 1 tbsp | dried oregano | 15 mL |
| | Hot pepper flakes to taste | |
| 1/4 cup | grated Parmesan cheese | 50 mL |
| | Fresh chopped parsley | |

1. In a large saucepan, heat oil over medium heat. Add garlic and cook until golden. Stir in olives, anchovies and capers; cook 1 minute. Add tomatoes, stirring to break up; reduce heat to medium-low and cook 20 minutes.

2. Meanwhile, in large pot of boiling salted water, cook fettuccine 8 to 10 minutes or until *al dente*; drain.

3. Stir calamari, basil, oregano and hot pepper flakes into sauce; cook just until calamari done, about 3 minutes. Toss sauce with drained pasta. Serve immediately, sprinkled with Parmesan and parsley.

*Upstairs at the Pudding*

*Boston*

FETTUCCINE WITH SCALLOPS AND SMOKED SALMON (PAGE 79) ➤

OVERLEAF: FETTUCCINE WITH MUSSELS, SHRIMP AND PARSLEY (PAGE 93) ➤

# Linguine with Curried Seafood

SERVES 4 TO 6

**TIP**

If the fishmonger hasn't already done so, remove the small muscle on the side of each scallop; it toughens as it cooks.

If you like curry increase the curry powder — up to 1/4 cup (50 mL) may be used.

| | | |
|---|---|---|
| 1/4 cup | butter | 50 mL |
| 1 1/2 cups | chopped onions | 375 mL |
| 1/2 cup | finely chopped carrots | 125 mL |
| 1/2 cup | chopped celery | 125 mL |
| 1 tbsp | minced garlic | 15 mL |
| 1 1/2 cups | diced green apple (unpeeled) | 375 mL |
| 3/4 cup | chopped tomatoes | 175 mL |
| 1/2 tsp | dried thyme | 2 mL |
| 1 | bay leaf | 1 |
| 1/4 cup | all-purpose flour | 50 mL |
| 2 tbsp | curry powder, or to taste | 25 mL |
| 2 cups | hot chicken stock | 500 mL |
| 1/4 cup | whipping (35%) cream | 50 mL |
| 1 lb | linguine or tagliatelle | 500 g |
| 1/3 cup | butter | 75 mL |
| 8 oz | mushrooms, chopped | 250 g |
| 8 oz | medium shrimp, peeled, deveined and cut in half | 250 g |
| 8 oz | scallops | 250 g |

1. In saucepan melt butter over medium heat. Add onions, carrots, celery and garlic; cook until soft, about 10 minutes. Stir in apple, tomatoes, thyme and bay leaf; cook 5 minutes. Reduce heat to low; add flour and curry powder and cook, stirring, 3 minutes. Stir in chicken stock; cook, uncovered, 15 minutes. Stir in cream; cook 3 minutes. Strain sauce into another saucepan, pressing vegetables with back of a spoon to squeeze out liquid; set strained sauce aside and discard vegetables.

2. In a large pot of boiling water, cook linguine 8 to 10 minutes or until *al dente*. Meanwhile, in a large skillet melt butter over medium-high heat. Add mushrooms and cook 3 minutes. Stir in shrimp and scallops; cook until seafood is just barely cooked. Stir in curry sauce.

3. Toss drained pasta with sauce. Serve immediately.

*Cafe des Artistes
New York*

≺ ANGEL HAIR PASTA WITH TOMATO AND SEAFOOD (PAGE 101)

# Capellini with Seafood

SERVES 4 TO 6

**TIP**

If fresh clams are unavailable, substitute with more mussels.

Discard any clams or mussels that do not open.

If the fish market hasn't already done so, remove the small muscle on the side of each scallop; it toughens as it cooks.

| | | |
|---|---|---|
| 1/4 cup | olive oil | 50 mL |
| 8 oz | plum tomatoes, diced | 250 g |
| 2 tsp | minced garlic | 10 mL |
| Pinch | cayenne pepper | Pinch |
| 6 oz | scallops | 175 g |
| 6 oz | shrimp, peeled and deveined | 175 g |
| 15 | clams | 15 |
| 10 | mussels | 10 |
| 12 oz | capellini or angel hair pasta | 375 g |
| 1/2 cup | clam juice or fish stock | 125 mL |
| 1/2 cup | chicken stock | 125 mL |
| 2 tbsp | chopped fresh parsley | 25 mL |

1. In a large saucepan, heat olive oil over medium heat. Add tomatoes, garlic and cayenne; cook until tomatoes are soft, about 5 minutes. Stir in scallops, shrimp, clams and mussels; cook, stirring constantly, just until shells open, about 5 minutes.

2. Meanwhile, in a large pot of boiling salted water, cook capellini 6 to 8 minutes or until *al dente*; drain. Add clam juice, chicken stock and parsley to sauce; bring to a boil. Toss pasta with sauce. Serve immediately.

— *Il Mulino* —
*New York*

# Linguine with Shrimp and Sun-Dried Tomatoes

**SERVES 4 TO 6**

**TIP**

It's more economical to buy dry-packed sun-dried tomatoes and rehydrate them yourself than to buy oil-packed. To rehydrate, bring a pan of water to a boil, add sun-dried tomatoes, reduce heat and simmer 5 minutes. Drain and use immediately, or put in a jar, add olive oil to cover, and refrigerate for later use.

| | | |
|---|---|---|
| 8 | asparagus spears, cut into 1-inch (2.5 cm) pieces | 8 |
| 12 oz | linguine or fettuccine | 375 g |
| 1/4 cup | butter | 50 mL |
| 1/2 cup | chopped onions | 125 mL |
| 2 tbsp | chopped shallots | 25 mL |
| 10 oz | shrimp, peeled, deveined and chopped | 300 g |
| 6 | drained, sun-dried tomatoes packed in oil, chopped | 6 |
| 1 cup | whipping (35%) cream | 250 mL |
| 1/4 cup | grated Parmesan cheese | 50 mL |

1. In pot of boiling water, blanch asparagus pieces for 2 minutes; refresh under cold water and drain. Set aside.
2. In a large pot of boiling salted water, cook linguine 8 to 10 minutes or until *al dente*. Meanwhile, prepare the sauce.
3. In a large skillet, melt butter over medium–high heat. Add onions and shallots; cook until golden. Stir in asparagus, shrimp and sun-dried tomatoes; cook just until shrimp turns pink. Stir in cream; cook until sauce thickens, about 2 minutes. Stir in Parmesan.
4. Toss drained pasta with sauce. Serve immediately.

*Il Nido / Il Monello*
*New York*

# Capellini with Asparagus and Scallops

**SERVES 4 TO 6**

**TIP**

If the fish market hasn't already done so, remove the small muscle on the side of each scallop; it toughens as it cooks.

| | | |
|---|---|---|
| 2 tbsp | olive oil | 25 mL |
| 3 | cloves garlic, crushed | 3 |
| 2 | green onions, chopped | 2 |
| 8 oz | asparagus, chopped | 250 g |
| 5 | plum tomatoes, chopped | 5 |
| 2 tbsp | chopped fresh basil (or 1 tsp [5 mL] dried) | 25 mL |
| 12 oz | capellini, angel hair pasta or spaghettini | 375 g |
| 1 lb | scallops | 500 g |
| | Salt and pepper to taste | |
| 1/4 cup | grated Parmesan cheese (optional) | 50 mL |

1. In a large skillet, heat olive oil over medium-high heat. Add garlic, green onions, asparagus, tomatoes and basil; cook, stirring, 5 minutes. Add 1/2 cup (125 mL) water; cook until tomatoes are well-blended, about 5 minutes.

2. Meanwhile, in large pot of boiling salted water, cook capellini 6 to 8 minutes or until *al dente*; drain. Stir scallops into sauce; cook until just barely done. Toss pasta with sauce; season to taste with salt and pepper. Serve immediately, sprinkled with Parmesan if desired.

*— Paola's —*
*New York*

# *Angel Hair Pasta with Tomato and Seafood*

**SERVES 6**

**TIP**

Use a combination of seafood — clams, mussels, scallops or shrimp.

| | | |
|---|---|---|
| 1/2 cup | white wine | 125 mL |
| 1/2 cup | olive oil | 125 mL |
| 3 tbsp | minced fresh basil (or 2 tsp [10 mL] dried) | 45 mL |
| 2 tbsp | minced fresh oregano (or 1 tsp [5 mL] dried) | 25 mL |
| 2 tbsp | minced fresh rosemary (or 1 tsp [5 mL] dried) | 25 mL |
| 2 tbsp | minced fresh sage (or 1/2 tsp [2 mL] dried) | 25 mL |
| 4 | cloves garlic, crushed | 4 |
| 1 1/2 lb | plum tomatoes, diced | 750 g |
| 12 oz | angel hair pasta or spaghettini | 375 g |
| 1 lb | cooked mixed seafood, cut into small pieces | 500 g |

1. In a saucepan combine wine, olive oil, basil, oregano, rosemary, sage and garlic; bring to a boil, reduce heat to low, cover and cook 10 minutes. Strain, returning liquid to saucepan and discarding solids. Stir in tomatoes; cook, stirring occasionally, over medium heat until it reaches sauce-like consistency, about 20 minutes.

2. Meanwhile, in large pot of boiling salted water, cook angel hair pasta 6 to 8 minutes or until *al dente*; drain. Stir seafood into sauce. Toss pasta with sauce. Serve immediately.

— *Palio* —
*New York*

# *Linguine with Baby Clams in Tomato Sauce*

**SERVES 4**

| | | |
|---|---|---|
| 1/3 cup | oil | 75 mL |
| 1 cup | chopped onions | 250 mL |
| 2 cups | canned tomatoes and juice, crushed | 500 mL |
| 2 tbsp | chopped fresh basil (or 1 1/2 tsp [7 mL] dried) | 25 mL |
| 1 tbsp | chopped fresh parsley | 15 mL |
| 12 oz | linguine | 375 g |
| 1 | can (5 oz [142 g]) baby clams, drained | 1 |
| | Grated Parmesan cheese | |

1. In a large skillet, heat oil over medium heat. Add onions and cook until soft. Stir in tomatoes, basil and parsley; reduce heat to low and cook until thickened, about 15 minutes.

2. Meanwhile, in a large pot of boiling salted water, cook linguine 8 to 10 minutes or until *al dente*; drain. Stir clams into sauce. Toss pasta with sauce. Serve immediately, sprinkled with Parmesan.

*Cafe de Medici*
*Vancouver*

# *Baked* OR *Stuffed* PASTA

# *Artichoke-Filled Pasta with Tomato Sauce*

**TIP**

The greener the tomatoes, the better this sauce will be.

Instead of canned, drained artichoke hearts, cook your own. Trim the leaves and choke from 5 artichokes. Thinly slice hearts. In a saucepan melt 1 tbsp (15 mL) butter over medium-low heat; cook sliced artichoke hearts, covered, until tender when pierced with the tip of a knife, about 10 minutes.

To make stuffing shells easier, carefully cut up one side with a pair of scissors; lay flat, stuff and roll.

*Primi / Valentino*
*Los Angeles*

**Preheat oven to 350° F (180° C)**

**13- by 9-inch (3 L) baking dish**

| | | |
|---|---|---|
| 12 | cannelloni or manicotti shells | 12 |
| 2 tbsp | olive oil | 25 mL |
| 1/4 cup | chopped onions | 50 mL |
| 1 | clove garlic, crushed | 1 |
| 1 | can (14 oz [398 mL]) artichoke hearts, drained and thinly sliced | 1 |
| 3 tbsp | white wine | 45 mL |
| 1/2 cup | ricotta cheese | 125 mL |
| 2 oz | Gorgonzola cheese | 50 g |
| 1 tsp | chopped fresh parsley | 5 mL |
| 1 | egg yolk | 1 |

**SAUCE:**

| | | |
|---|---|---|
| 2 tbsp | olive oil | 25 mL |
| 1/2 cup | finely chopped carrots | 125 mL |
| 1 | clove garlic, crushed | 1 |
| 1 lb | green tomatoes, coarsely chopped | 500 g |
| 1 cup | chicken stock | 250 mL |
| 1/4 cup | chopped fresh basil (or 1 tbsp [15 mL] dried) | 50 mL |
| 1 | bay leaf | 1 |
| | Salt and pepper to taste | |

1. In a large pot of boiling salted water, cook cannelloni shells 10 to 12 minutes or until tender; drain. Rinse under cold water, drain and set aside.

2. In a large skillet, heat olive oil over medium–high heat. Add onions and garlic; cook until softened. Stir in artichokes and white wine; cook until liquid evaporates, about 3 minutes. Transfer to a food processor; pulse on and off until chopped. Add ricotta, Gorgonzola, parsley and egg yolk to food processor; process until mixed. Stuff pasta shells and place in baking dish.

3. Make the sauce: In a saucepan heat olive oil over medium heat. Add carrots and garlic; cook 1 minute. Stir in tomatoes, chicken stock, basil and bay leaf; cook until thick, stirring occasionally, about 15 minutes. Remove bay leaf; season to taste with salt and pepper. Pour over cannelloni. Cover dish tightly with aluminum foil.

4. Bake until hot, about 20 to 25 minutes.

# *Lasagne with Bell Peppers, Eggplant and Zucchini*

**Preheat broiler**

**13- by 9-inch (3 L) baking dish**

**SERVES 8**

**TIP**

Always cook an additional lasagne noodle or two; it will give you a sample to taste for doneness, and you will have extra if any tear.

Lasagne cuts into portions more easily if you let it stand 10 minutes before serving.

*Locanda Veneta*
*Los Angeles*

| | | |
|---|---|---|
| 9 | lasagne noodles | 9 |
| 2 | red or yellow peppers | 2 |
| 1/3 cup | olive oil | 75 mL |
| 1 | zucchini, halved lengthwise and thinly sliced | 1 |
| 1 | small eggplant, halved lengthwise and thinly sliced | 1 |
| | Flour for dusting vegetables | |
| 2 tbsp | olive oil | 25 mL |
| 8 oz | mushrooms, sliced | 250 g |
| 1/4 cup | chopped onions | 50 mL |
| 3 cups | prepared tomato sauce | 750 mL |
| 12 oz | mozzarella cheese, sliced | 375 g |
| 1/2 cup | grated Parmesan cheese | 125 mL |

1. In a large pot of boiling salted water, cook lasagne noodles 6 to 8 minutes or until tender; drain. Rinse under cold water, drain and set aside.

2. Broil peppers in oven, turning often, for 15 minutes or until charred. Cool. Peel skins, remove stem and seeds, and cut into strips; set aside.

3. In a large skillet, heat 1/3 cup (75 mL) olive oil over medium-high heat. Dust zucchini and eggplant slices with flour. Keeping zucchini and eggplant separate, cook vegetables in batches until barely cooked; remove from pan and set aside. Add 2 tbsp (25 mL) olive oil to pan; cook mushrooms and onions until soft and set aside.

4. Preheat oven to 350° F (180° C). Spread 3/4 cup (175 mL) of the tomato sauce in bottom of baking dish. Arrange three noodles in dish. Layer with all the eggplant, half of the pepper strips, half of the mozzarella, half of the Parmesan and 1 cup (250 mL) of the tomato sauce. Arrange three noodles over top. Layer with zucchini, mushroom mixture, remaining pepper strips and remaining mozzarella. Top with remaining noodles, tomato sauce and Parmesan cheese. Cover dish tightly with aluminum foil.

5. Bake until hot, about 45 minutes.

# Spinach and Ricotta–Filled Cannelloni in a Vegetable Sauce

**Preheat oven to 350° F (180° C)**

**13- by 9-inch (3 L) baking dish**

SERVES 4 TO 6

TIP

For extra color, substitute yellow summer squash for one of the zucchini.

To make stuffing shells easier, carefully cut up one side with a pair of scissors; lay flat, stuff and roll.

| | | |
|---|---|---|
| 12 | cannelloni or manicotti shells | 12 |
| Half | package (10 oz [300 g]) frozen spinach, thawed | Half |
| 1 1/4 cups | ricotta cheese | 300 mL |
| 3/4 cup | grated Parmesan cheese | 175 mL |
| 1 | egg yolk | 1 |
| 1/4 tsp | nutmeg | 1 mL |
| 1 | carrot, finely diced | 1 |
| 2 | small zucchini, finely diced | 2 |
| 1/2 cup | butter | 125 mL |
| 2 tbsp | chopped fresh basil (or 1 tsp [5 mL] dried) | 25 mL |
| 3 tbsp | grated Parmesan cheese | 45 mL |

1. In a large pot of boiling salted water, cook cannelloni 10 to 12 minutes or until tender; drain. Rinse under cold water, drain and set aside.

2. In small saucepan, bring 1/2 cup (125 mL) water to a boil; stir in spinach, cover, reduce heat to medium and cook 5 minutes. Drain and squeeze out excess liquid. Chop finely. In a bowl combine spinach, ricotta, Parmesan, egg yolk and nutmeg. Stuff shells and place in baking dish.

3. Bring a small saucepan of water to a boil; cook carrot and zucchini 1 minute. Drain. In a large skillet, melt 1/4 cup (50 mL) of the butter over medium-high heat. Add drained carrot and zucchini and basil; cook 3 minutes. Stir in 1 1/2 cups (375 mL) water; bring to a boil and cook until liquid is reduced by half, about 5 minutes. Stir in remaining butter; cook until slightly thickened, about 2 minutes. Remove from heat and stir in Parmesan. Pour over cannelloni.

4. Cover dish tightly with aluminum foil. Bake until hot, about 20 to 30 minutes.

*The Donatello*
*San Francisco*

# Pasta Shells Stuffed with Cheese in a Creamy Tomato Sauce

**SERVES 4 TO 5**

**TIP**

Ricotta cheese is available in 5% and 10% fat — to reduce fat use the 5%

Always cook an additional pasta shell or two; it will give you a sample to taste for doneness, and you will have extra if any tear.

**Preheat oven to 375° F (190° C)**

**13- by 9-inch (3 L) baking dish**

| | | |
|---|---|---|
| 1/4 cup | whipping (35%) cream | 50 mL |
| 8 oz | jumbo pasta shells or 12 manicotti shells | 250 g |
| 1 cup | ricotta cheese | 250 mL |
| 1/2 cup | grated Parmesan cheese | 125 mL |
| 1/4 cup | finely chopped chives or green onions | 50 mL |
| 1/4 cup | shredded Havarti, brick or fontina cheese | 50 mL |
| 2 | egg yolks | 2 |
| 2 cups | prepared tomato sauce | 500 mL |
| 1/3 cup | grated Parmesan cheese | 75 mL |
| | Chopped chives | |

1. Butter bottom of baking dish. Pour cream into dish.
2. In a large pot of boiling salted water, cook jumbo pasta shells 8 to 10 minutes or until tender; drain. Rinse under cold water, drain and set aside.
3. In a bowl, stir together ricotta, Parmesan, chives, Havarti and egg yolks. Stuff pasta shells and place in baking dish. Pour tomato sauce over shells; sprinkle with Parmesan. Cover dish tightly with aluminum foil.
4. Bake until heated through, about 20 minutes. Serve sprinkled with chopped chives.

*Umberto al Porto*
*Vancouver*

# Scallop-and-Mushroom-Stuffed Shells

**SERVES 4 TO 6**

**Preheat oven to 350° F (180° C)**

**13- by 9-inch (3 L) baking dish**

**TIP**

If the fish market hasn't already done so, remove the small muscle on the side of each scallop; it toughens as it cooks.

Always cook an additional pasta shell or two; it will give you a sample to taste for doneness, and you will have extra if any tear.

| | | |
|---|---|---|
| 20 | jumbo pasta shells | 20 |
| 2 tbsp | olive oil | 25 mL |
| 8 oz | scallops | 250 g |
| 1/2 cup | chopped onions | 125 mL |
| 8 oz | mushrooms, coarsely chopped (preferably wild, such as oyster or shiitake) | 250 g |
| 1 | sprig fresh thyme (or pinch dried) | 1 |
| 1 | tomato, diced | 1 |
| **SAUCE:** | | |
| 1 tsp | olive oil | 5 mL |
| 3 tbsp | chopped shallots or onions | 45 mL |
| 6 | whole peppercorns | 6 |
| 1 | sprig fresh thyme (or pinch dried) | 1 |
| Pinch | saffron | Pinch |
| 1/2 cup | white wine | 125 mL |
| 2 tbsp | brandy | 25 mL |
| 1 cup | chicken or fish stock | 250 mL |
| 1 tbsp | soft butter | 15 mL |
| 1 1/2 tsp | all-purpose flour | 7 mL |

*The Donatello
San Francisco*

1. In a large pot of boiling salted water, cook jumbo pasta shells 8 to 10 minutes or until tender; drain. Rinse under cold water, drain and set aside.

2. In a skillet heat 1 tbsp (15 mL) of the olive oil over medium-high heat; add scallops and cook just until barely done. Remove from skillet; set aside to cool. Add remaining oil to skillet; cook onions until softened. Stir in mushrooms and thyme; cook until vegetables are soft. Remove from heat. Stir in tomato. Chop cooled scallops and add to vegetable mixture. Once cool, stuff shells and put in baking dish.

3. Make the sauce: In a saucepan heat oil over medium heat. Add shallots, peppercorns, thyme and saffron; cook 2 minutes. Stir in wine and brandy; bring to a boil and cook until liquid reduced by half, about 3 minutes. Stir in chicken stock, reduce heat to medium and cook 5 minutes. Meanwhile, in a small bowl, combine butter and flour to form a smooth paste. Stir into sauce and cook until sauce thickens, about 1 minute. Strain sauce; pour over stuffed shells.

4. Cover dish tightly with aluminum foil. Bake until hot, about 20 minutes.

# Tortellini with Cheesy Tomato Sauce

**SERVES 4**

**TIP**

Use cheese tortellini instead of meat tortellini; or use ravioli or agnolotti.

Instead of store-bought, try your own homemade tortellini.

**Preheat oven to 500° F (260° C)**

**8-cup (2 L) casserole**

| | | |
|---|---|---|
| 1 lb | frozen or fresh meat–stuffed tortellini | 500 g |
| 1 cup | whipping (35%) cream | 250 mL |
| 1/2 cup | prepared tomato sauce | 125 mL |
| 1/4 cup | grated Parmesan cheese | 50 mL |
| 1 tbsp | chopped fresh parsley | 15 mL |
| | Salt and pepper to taste | |
| 2 tbsp | grated Parmesan cheese | 25 mL |

1. In a large pot of boiling salted water, cook tortellini according to package directions or until *al dente*; drain.

2. In a large saucepan, combine cream, tomato sauce, 1/4 cup (50 mL) Parmesan and parsley; bring to a boil, reduce heat to low and cook 5 minutes. Add tortellini and cook 3 minutes. Season to taste with salt and pepper. Transfer to casserole. Sprinkle with Parmesan.

3. Bake just until cheese starts to brown, about 4 minutes. Serve immediately.

*On Broadway Ristorante*

*Fort Worth*

# Mushrooms and Cheese in Pasta Shells

**Preheat oven to 350° F (180° C)**

**8-inch (2 L) square baking dish**

| | | |
|---|---|---|
| 8 oz | jumbo pasta shells | 250 g |
| 1/4 cup | olive oil | 50 mL |
| 2 tbsp | minced garlic | 25 mL |
| 1 lb | mushrooms, chopped | 500 g |
| 1/4 cup | chopped green onions | 50 mL |
| 1 cup | grated Parmesan cheese | 250 mL |

**SAUCE:**

| | | |
|---|---|---|
| 1/2 cup | Marsala wine or other sweet red wine | 125 mL |
| 1 tbsp | chopped shallots | 15 mL |
| 1/2 cup | whipping (35%) cream | 125 mL |
| 1/3 cup | soft butter | 75 mL |
| 1/2 cup | chopped tomatoes | 125 mL |
| 1/4 cup | fresh or frozen green peas | 50 mL |
| 1/4 cup | sliced mushrooms, preferably wild | 50 mL |
| | Salt and pepper to taste | |

1. In a large pot of boiling salted water, cook jumbo pasta shells 8 to 10 minutes or until tender; drain. Rinse under cold water, drain and set aside.

2. In a large skillet, heat oil over medium heat. Add garlic and mushrooms; cook until soft. Stir in green onions; cook 2 minutes. Transfer to food processor; purée with Parmesan. Stuff shells and put in baking dish.

3. Make the sauce: In a small saucepan, combine Marsala and shallots; bring to a boil, reduce heat to medium and cook 2 minutes. Stir in cream; cook 2 minutes longer. Stir in butter until blended. Add tomatoes, green peas and mushrooms; season to taste with salt and pepper. Pour over shells.

4. Cover dish tightly with aluminum foil. Bake until hot, about 30 minutes.

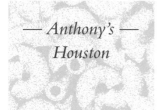

*— Anthony's —
Houston*

# Salmon Cannelloni with Creamy White Sauce

**SERVES 4 TO 5**

**TIP**

To make stuffing shells easier, carefully cut up one side with a pair of scissors; lay flat, stuff and roll.

**Preheat oven to 350° F (180° C)**

**13- by 9-inch (3 L) baking dish**

| | | |
|---|---|---|
| 10 | cannelloni or manicotti shells | 10 |
| 1/4 cup | butter | 50 mL |
| 1/3 cup | chopped shallots or onions | 75 mL |
| 1 1/2 tsp | drained capers | 7 mL |
| 8 oz | salmon fillets, skinned, boned and cubed | 250 g |
| 1/4 cup | chopped fresh dill (or 1 tbsp [15 mL] dried) | 50 mL |
| 4 tsp | brandy or cognac | 20 mL |
| 1/2 cup | whipping (35%) cream | 125 mL |
| **SAUCE:** | | |
| 4 tsp | white wine | 20 mL |
| 4 tsp | white wine vinegar | 20 mL |
| 1 tbsp | minced shallots or onions | 15 mL |
| 1 tsp | minced garlic | 5 mL |
| 1/3 cup | whipping (35%) cream | 75 mL |
| 1/3 cup | soft butter | 75 mL |
| 1 tbsp | chopped fresh dill (or 1/2 tsp [2 mL] dried) | 15 mL |
| 2 tsp | freshly squeezed lemon juice | 10 mL |
| | Salt and pepper to taste | |

1. In a large pot of boiling salted water, cook cannelloni 10 to 12 minutes or until tender; drain. Rinse under cold water, drain and set aside.
2. In a large skillet, melt butter over medium-high heat. Cook shallots and capers 1 minute. Add salmon; cook until just barely done. Stir in dill and brandy; cook 2 minutes longer. Transfer to food processor; purée with cream. Stuff shells and put in baking dish.

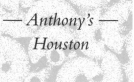

*— Anthony's —*
*Houston*

3. Make the sauce: In a saucepan over medium heat, combine white wine, white wine vinegar and shallots; cook 1 minute. Stir in garlic and cream; cook 1 minute longer. Stir in butter; cook until combined. Stir in dill and lemon juice; season to taste with salt and pepper. Pour over shells.

4. Cover dish tightly with aluminum foil. Bake until hot, about 25 minutes.

# Cannelloni with Cheese and Meat Filling

SERVES 4

**TIP**

To make stuffing shells easier, carefully cut up one side with a pair of scissors; lay flat, stuff and roll.

**Preheat oven to 350° F (180° C)**

**13- by 9-inch (3 L) baking dish**

| | | |
|---|---|---|
| 10 | cannelloni or manicotti shells | 10 |
| 2 tbsp | olive oil | 25 mL |
| 3 oz | ground beef | 75 g |
| 3 oz | ground veal | 75 g |
| 2 tbsp | finely chopped onions | 25 mL |
| 1 tbsp | finely chopped carrots | 15 mL |
| 1 tbsp | finely chopped celery | 15 mL |
| 1 tsp | minced garlic | 5 mL |
| 1/4 cup | red wine | 50 mL |
| 1 tbsp | tomato paste | 15 mL |
| 2 oz | mozzarella cheese, shredded | 50 g |
| 2 tbsp | ricotta cheese | 25 mL |
| 1 tbsp | grated Parmesan cheese | 15 mL |
| Pinch | nutmeg | Pinch |
| Pinch | dried sage | Pinch |
| Pinch | dried rosemary | Pinch |
| | Salt and pepper to taste | |
| 1 | egg | 1 |
| 1 1/2 cups | prepared tomato sauce | 375 mL |
| | Grated Parmesan cheese to taste | |

1. In a large pot of boiling salted water, cook cannelloni 10 to 12 minutes or until tender; drain. Rinse under cold water, drain and set aside.
2. In a skillet heat olive oil over medium–high heat. Add beef and veal; cook, stirring, until no longer pink. Stir in onions, carrots, celery and garlic; cook until vegetables are soft. Stir in red wine and tomato paste; bring to a boil and cook 2 minutes. Remove from heat; cool slightly. Stir in mozzarella, ricotta, Parmesan, nutmeg, sage and rosemary; season to taste with salt and pepper. Stir in egg. Stuff shells and put in baking dish.

*Andrea's Restaurant*
*New Orleans*

3.  Pour tomato sauce over shells. Sprinkle with Parmesan. Cover dish tightly with aluminum foil. Bake until hot, about 30 minutes.

# Baked Penne with Mushrooms and Cheese

**SERVES 4 TO 6**

**Preheat oven to 400° F (200° C)**

**12-cup (3 L) casserole**

| | | |
|---|---|---|
| 12 oz | penne | 375 g |
| 3 tbsp | butter | 45 mL |
| 1 lb | mushrooms (preferably wild), thinly sliced | 500 g |
| 3 | cloves garlic, crushed | 3 |
| Pinch | hot pepper flakes | Pinch |
| 6 oz | Swiss cheese, shredded | 175 g |
| 6 oz | Havarti, brick or Bel Paese cheese, shredded | 175 g |
| 1/3 cup | grated Parmesan cheese | 75 mL |
| 1 cup | whipping (35%) cream | 250 mL |
| | Freshly ground pepper | |

1. In a large pot of boiling salted water, cook penne 8 to 10 minutes or until *al dente*; drain.
2. In a large skillet, melt butter over medium-high heat. Add mushrooms, garlic and hot pepper flakes; cook 3 minutes.
3. In a bowl combine Swiss, Havarti and Parmesan cheeses.
4. Cover bottom of casserole with one quarter of the pasta. Spread one quarter of the mushroom mixture on top, followed by one quarter of the cheese mixture. Repeat layers three times. Pour cream over top. Sprinkle with pepper.
5. Cover casserole tightly with aluminum foil. Bake 12 minutes. Remove foil and bake until a light brown crust forms on top, about 12 minutes longer.

*— Tony's —*
*Houston*

# Tortellini with Walnut Pesto

**TIP**

Use your own homemade tortellini, ravioli or agnolotti instead of store-bought.

You can use this walnut pesto over any of your favorite pastas.

It's more economical to buy dry-packed sun-dried tomatoes and rehydrate them yourself than to buy oil-packed. To rehydrate, bring a pan of water to a boil, add sun-dried tomatoes, reduce heat and simmer 5 minutes. Drain and use immediately, or put in a jar, add olive oil to cover, and refrigerate for later use.

For maximum flavor, toast the walnuts in a 350° F (180° C) oven until fragrant, about 10 minutes.

| | | |
|---|---|---|
| 1 lb | frozen or fresh spinach and cheese-stuffed tortellini or ravioli | 500 g |
| 1 cup | walnut pieces | 250 mL |
| 1/4 cup | grated Romano or Parmesan cheese | 50 mL |
| 1 tsp | minced garlic | 5 mL |
| 1 cup | whipping (35%) cream | 250 mL |
| 1/2 cup | drained, sun-dried tomatoes packed in oil, thinly sliced | 125 mL |

1. In a large pot of boiling salted water, cook tortellini according to package directions or until *al dente*. Meanwhile, prepare the sauce.

2. In food processor, grind walnuts, Romano and garlic until finely chopped. In a saucepan, heat cream over medium heat. Stir in walnut mixture; cook 2 minutes.

3. Toss drained tortellini with sauce. Serve immediately, garnished with sun-dried tomatoes.

— *Spiaggia* —
*Chicago*

# Pine Nut Cannelloni

**TIP**

To make stuffing shells easier, carefully cut up one side with a pair of scissors; lay flat, stuff and roll.

Use this filling to make your own home-made ravioli, tortellini, etc.

To toast pine nuts, bake in a 350° F (180° C) oven until fragrant, about 10 minutes.

**Preheat oven to 350° F (180° C)**

**13- by 9-inch (3 L) baking dish**

| | | |
|---|---|---:|
| 12 | cannelloni or manicotti shells | 12 |
| 1 1/4 cups | ricotta cheese | 300 mL |
| 1/2 cup | toasted pine nuts | 125 mL |
| 1/2 tsp | minced fresh sage (or 1/8 tsp [0.5 mL] dried) | 2 mL |
| | Salt and pepper to taste | |

**SAUCE:**

| | | |
|---|---|---:|
| 1/4 cup | butter | 50 mL |
| 1 tbsp | butter | 15 mL |
| 1/2 cup | chopped onions | 125 mL |
| 1/2 cup | chicken stock | 125 mL |
| 1/3 cup | whipping (35%) cream | 75 mL |
| 1 tbsp | sweet sherry | 15 mL |

1.  In a large pot of boiling salted water, cook cannelloni 10 to 12 minutes or until tender; drain. Rinse under cold water, drain and set aside.

2.  In a bowl stir together ricotta, pine nuts and sage; season to taste with salt and pepper. Stuff shells and put in baking dish.

3.  Make the sauce: In a small saucepan melt 1/4 cup (50 mL) butter over medium-high heat; cook until brown. Remove from heat. In skillet, melt 1 tbsp (15 mL) butter over medium heat; add onions and cook until soft. Stir in chicken stock, cream, sherry and browned butter; cook 3 minutes. Strain sauce and pour over cannelloni.

4.  Cover dish tightly with aluminum foil. Bake until hot, about 25 minutes.

*— Avanzare —*
*Chicago*

# Stuffed Pasta with Gorgonzola Cream Sauce

**TIP**

Use thinly sliced ham if prosciutto is unavailable.

Use your own home-made tortellini or ravioli instead of store-bought.

| | | |
|---|---|---|
| 1 lb | frozen or fresh cheese-stuffed tortellini or ravioli | 500 g |
| 3/4 cup | whipping (35%) cream | 175 mL |
| 4 oz | Gorgonzola cheese, cut in pieces | 125 g |
| 1/2 cup | grated Parmesan cheese | 125 mL |
| 3 | slices prosciutto, coarsely chopped | 3 |
| 1 tsp | minced fresh parsley | 5 mL |

1. In a large pot of boiling salted water, cook tortellini according to package directions or until *al dente*; drain.

2. In a large saucepan, cook cream and Gorgonzola over medium heat, stirring, until cheese melts, about 3 minutes. Stir in tortellini; cook 3 minutes longer. Stir in Parmesan. Serve immediately, sprinkled with prosciutto and parsley.

— *La Sila* —
*Montreal*

# Lamb Cannelloni with Walnut Parmesan Sauce

**Preheat oven to 375° F (190° C)**

**13- by 9-inch (3 L) baking dish**

| | | |
|---|---|---|
| 12 | cannelloni shells | 12 |
| 1 tbsp | olive oil | 15 mL |
| 8 oz | lamb, cut into cubes | 250 g |
| 1 tbsp | chopped fresh rosemary (or 1 tsp [5 mL] dried) | 15 mL |
| 1 tsp | minced garlic | 5 mL |
| 1/2 cup | chopped onions | 125 mL |
| 2 tbsp | chopped fresh parsley (or 1 1/2 tsp [7 mL] dried) | 25 mL |
| 1/4 cup | seasoned bread crumbs | 50 mL |
| | Salt and pepper to taste | |
| 1 | egg | 1 |

**SAUCE:**

| | | |
|---|---|---|
| 2 tbsp | butter | 25 mL |
| 1 cup | whipping (35%) cream | 250 mL |
| 2 tbsp | grated Parmesan cheese | 25 mL |
| 2 tsp | minced fresh parsley | 10 mL |
| 2 tsp | finely chopped toasted walnuts | 10 mL |

1. In a large pot of boiling salted water, cook cannelloni 10 to 12 minutes or until tender; drain. Rinse under cold water, drain and set aside.

2. In a large skillet, heat oil over medium–high heat. Add lamb, rosemary, garlic and onions; cook until lamb is medium done. Stir in parsley. Transfer to a food processor; purée with bread crumbs. Season to taste with salt and pepper. Add egg; process until well-mixed. Stuff shells and place in baking dish.

3. Make the sauce: In a saucepan bring butter, cream, Parmesan, parsley and walnuts to a boil; pour over shells. Cover dish tightly with aluminum foil.

4. Bake until hot, about 15 minutes.

*The Brass Elephant*
*Baltimore*

# *Ricotta-Stuffed Pasta Shells with Mushroom Sauce*

**SERVES 4 TO 6**

**TIP**

Cook an additional pasta shell or two; it will give you a sample to taste for doneness, and you will have extra if any tear.

**Preheat oven to 375° F (190° C)**

**13- by 9-inch (3 L) baking dish**

| | | |
|---|---|---|
| 16 | jumbo pasta shells | 16 |
| 1 tbsp | olive oil | 15 mL |
| 2 | green onions, finely chopped | 2 |
| 1 | bunch watercress, stemmed | 1 |
| 1 lb | ricotta cheese | 500 g |
| 1 tbsp | minced fresh parsley (or 1 1/2 tsp [7 mL] dried) | 15 mL |
| | Salt and pepper to taste | |
| 1 | egg | 1 |

**SAUCE:**

| | | |
|---|---|---|
| 2 cups | beef or veal stock | 500 mL |
| 1 1/2 cups | sliced mushrooms, preferably wild (such as shiitake) | 375 mL |
| 1 tbsp | minced fresh basil (or 1/2 tsp [2 mL] dried) | 15 mL |
| 2 | sprigs fresh thyme (or 1/2 tsp [2 mL] dried) | 2 |
| 4 tsp | grated Parmesan or Romano cheese | 20 mL |

1. In a large pot of boiling salted water, cook jumbo pasta shells 8 to 10 minutes or until tender; drain. Rinse under cold water, drain and set aside.

2. In a large skillet, heat oil over medium–high heat. Add green onions and watercress; cook just until wilted. Cool and chop finely. In a bowl, combine chopped vegetables, ricotta and parsley; season to taste with salt and pepper. Stir in egg. Stuff shells and put in baking dish.

3. Make the sauce: In saucepan bring stock to a boil; boil until reduced by half, about 5 minutes. Stir in mushrooms, basil, thyme and Parmesan; boil 1 minute longer. Pour over shells.

4. Cover dish tightly with aluminum foil. Bake until hot, about 20 minutes.

*The Brass Elephant Baltimore*

# Tortellini with Creamy Cheese Sauce

**SERVES 4**

**TIP**

Use ricotta or cream cheese if mascarpone is unavailable.

Use your own homemade tortellini or ravioli instead of store-bought.

| | | |
|---|---|---|
| 12 oz | frozen or fresh spinach and cheese-stuffed tortellini or ravioli | 375 g |
| 1 cup | whipping (35%) cream | 250 mL |
| 1/4 cup | mascarpone cheese | 50 mL |
| 3 tbsp | grated Parmesan cheese | 45 mL |
| 2 tbsp | butter | 25 mL |
| Pinch | nutmeg | Pinch |
| | Salt and pepper to taste | |

1. In a large pot of boiling salted water, cook tortellini according to package directions or until *al dente*; drain.
2. In a saucepan bring cream to a boil. Stir in mascarpone, Parmesan, butter and nutmeg; boil 2 minutes, stirring. Season to taste with salt and pepper.
3. Toss tortellini with sauce. Serve immediately.

*— Galileo —*
*Washington*

# *Pasta Filled with Chicken and Ricotta Cheese*

**SERVES 4 TO 6**

**Preheat oven to 350° F (180° C)**

**8-inch (2 L) square baking dish**

**TIP**

Cook an additional pasta shell or two; it will give you a sample to taste for doneness, and you will have extra if any tear.

Instead of tomato sauce, use the mascarpone sauce from the previous recipe (Tortellini with Creamy Cheese Sauce, page 124).

| | | |
|---|---|---|
| 16 | jumbo pasta shells | 16 |
| 1 tbsp | olive oil | 15 mL |
| 6 oz | chicken breasts | 175 g |
| 1/3 cup | thawed frozen chopped spinach, well-packed | 75 mL |
| 1 1/2 cups | ricotta cheese | 375 mL |
| 1 tbsp | minced fresh parsley | 15 mL |
| | Salt and pepper to taste | |
| 2 | eggs | 2 |
| 1 cup | prepared tomato sauce | 250 mL |

1. In a large pot of boiling salted water, cook jumbo pasta shells 8 to 10 minutes or until tender; drain. Rinse under cold water, drain and set aside.

2. In a skillet heat oil over medium–high heat. Add chicken; cook until well-browned. Turn and cook other side until browned and cooked through. Remove from skillet and let cool. Cut into small pieces; set aside.

3. In a small saucepan of boiling water, cook spinach 2 minutes; drain and squeeze out excess moisture. In a bowl, combine spinach, chicken, ricotta and parsley; season to taste with salt and pepper. Stir in eggs. Stuff shells and put in baking dish.

4. Pour tomato sauce over shells. Cover dish tightly with aluminum foil. Bake until hot, about 30 minutes.

*Monte Carlo Living Room*

*Philadelphia*

# Pasta Rolls Filled with Smoked Salmon and Cheese

SERVES 4 TO 5

**Preheat oven to 350° F (180° C)**

**13- by 9-inch (3 L) baking dish**

| | | |
|---|---|---|
| 10 | manicotti shells | 10 |
| 1 1/4 cups | ricotta or cottage cheese | 300 mL |
| 4 oz | cooked chopped spinach, squeezed dry | 125 g |
| 4 oz | smoked salmon, chopped | 125 g |
| | Pepper to taste | |
| 2 cups | prepared tomato sauce | 500 mL |
| 1/2 cup | shredded Swiss cheese, preferably Gruyere | 125 mL |

1. In a large pot of boiling salted water, cook manicotti 10 to 12 minutes or until tender; drain. Rinse under cold water, drain and set aside.

2. In a bowl mix together ricotta, spinach and smoked salmon; season to taste with pepper. Stuff shells. Spread 1 cup (250 mL) of the tomato sauce on bottom of baking dish. Arrange manicotti in dish. Top with remaining tomato sauce. Sprinkle with Swiss cheese.

3. Cover dish tightly with aluminum foil. Bake until hot, about 25 minutes.

**TIP**

Ricotta cheese will give a smoother texture to the filling; if you use cottage cheese and want a creamy filling, purée it in the food processor.

To make stuffing shells easier, carefully cut up one side with a pair of scissors; lay flat, stuff and roll.

*— Movenpick —*
*Toronto*

# *Cheese and Pumpkin Cannelloni*

**TIP**

Use cream cheese or ricotta instead of mascarpone cheese.

Use this stuffing in your own homemade tortellini or ravioli.

To make stuffing shells easier, carefully cut up one side with a pair of scissors; lay flat, stuff and roll.

Preheat oven to 350° F (180° C)

13- by 9-inch (3 L) baking dish

| | | |
|---|---|---|
| 12 | cannelloni or manicotti shells | 12 |
| 1/4 cup | butter | 50 mL |
| 2 tbsp | olive oil | 25 mL |
| 1 cup | chopped onions | 250 mL |
| 1 cup | canned pumpkin | 250 mL |
| 1/3 cup | grated Parmesan cheese | 75 mL |
| 1/2 cup | mascarpone cheese | 125 mL |
| 1 1/2 tsp | fine bread crumbs | 7 mL |
| 2 | amaretti cookies, finely crushed | 2 |

**SAUCE:**

| | | |
|---|---|---|
| 1/4 cup | butter | 50 mL |
| 1/4 cup | whipping (35%) cream | 50 mL |
| 2 tbsp | chopped fresh sage (or 1/2 tsp [2 mL] dried) | 25 mL |

1. In a large pot of boiling salted water, cook cannelloni 10 to 12 minutes or until tender; drain. Rinse under cold water, drain and set aside.

2. In a skillet heat butter and oil over medium–high heat. Add onions and cook until golden brown. Remove from heat. Stir in pumpkin, Parmesan, mascarpone, bread crumbs and amaretti. Stuff shells and put in baking dish.

3. Make the sauce: In a saucepan bring butter, cream and sage to a boil. Pour over shells. Cover dish tightly with aluminum foil.

4. Bake until hot, about 20 minutes.

— *Cafe Trevi* —
*New York*

# *Ravioli with Nutty Cream Sauce*

**SERVES 3 TO 4**

**TIP**

For extra flavor toast the nuts in a 350° F (180° C) oven until golden and fragrant, about 8 minutes.

Instead of store-bought, use your own homemade ravioli or tortellini.

| | | |
|---|---|---|
| 12 oz | frozen or fresh ravioli or tortellini (any stuffing) | 375 g |
| 1/3 cup | finely chopped pine nuts | 75 mL |
| 1/4 cup | finely chopped hazelnuts | 50 mL |
| 2 tbsp | finely chopped walnuts | 25 mL |
| 3/4 cup | whipping (35%) cream | 175 mL |
| 2 tbsp | butter | 25 mL |
| | Salt and pepper to taste | |
| 1/4 cup | grated Parmesan cheese | 50 mL |

1. In a large pot of boiling salted water, cook ravioli according to package directions or until *al dente*; drain.
2. In a bowl combine pine nuts, hazelnuts and walnuts. In a large saucepan, combine cream, butter and half the nut mixture; bring to a boil. Stir in pasta; season to taste with salt and pepper. Serve immediately, sprinkled with remaining nuts and Parmesan cheese.

*— Il Cantino —*
*New York*

PASTA SHELLS STUFFED WITH CHEESE IN A CREAMY TOMATO SAUCE (PAGE 109)  ➤

*OVERLEAF:* ITALIAN RICE WITH SPRING VEGETABLES (PAGE 143)  ➤

# PASTA WITH *Basic Sauces*

≺ LASAGNE WITH BELL PEPPERS, EGGPLANT AND ZUCCHINI (PAGE 106)

# Bow Tie Pasta with Creamy Tomato Sauce

**SERVES 2 TO 4**

| | | |
|---|---|---|
| 8 oz | bow tie pasta (farfalle) | 250 g |
| 4 oz | medium spicy sausage, casings removed | 125 g |
| 1/2 cup | whipping (35%) cream | 125 mL |
| 1/2 cup | fresh or frozen green peas | 125 mL |
| 1/2 cup | prepared tomato sauce | 125 mL |
| 1/4 cup | butter | 50 mL |
| 1/4 cup | grated Parmesan cheese | 50 mL |

1. In a large pot of boiling salted water, cook bow tie pasta 8 to 10 minutes or until *al dente*. Meanwhile, prepare the sauce.

2. In a large skillet over medium-high heat, cook sausage meat, stirring to break up, until no longer pink, about 5 minutes. Stir in cream, peas, tomato sauce and butter; bring to a boil. Stir in Parmesan.

3. Toss drained pasta with sauce. Serve immediately.

*— Il Cantinori —*
*New York*

# *Penne with Pomodoro Sauce*

**SERVES 2 TO 4**

**TIP**

Use bacon if pancetta is unavailable.

| | | |
|---|---|---|
| 2 tbsp | olive oil | 25 mL |
| 1 tsp | minced garlic | 5 mL |
| 1 cup | finely chopped tomatoes, preferably plum | 250 mL |
| 1 tbsp | minced fresh basil (or 1/2 tsp [2 mL] dried) | 15 mL |
| | Salt and pepper to taste | |
| 8 oz | penne | 250 g |
| 2 tbsp | olive oil | 25 mL |
| 3 oz | pancetta, chopped | 75 g |
| 2 | cloves garlic, crushed | 2 |
| 1/2 tsp | dried oregano | 2 mL |
| 2 tbsp | white wine | 25 mL |
| 1/4 cup | butter | 50 mL |
| 1/4 cup | grated Parmesan cheese | 50 mL |

1.  In a skillet heat oil over medium heat. Add garlic and cook 1 minute. Stir in tomatoes and basil; cook 10 minutes. Season to taste with salt and pepper; set aside.

2.  In a large pot of boiling salted water, cook penne 8 to 10 minutes or until *al dente*. Meanwhile, prepare the sauce.

3.  In a large skillet, heat oil over medium–high heat. Add pancetta, garlic and oregano; cook until golden. Stir in wine. Add tomato sauce; cook 3 minutes. Stir in butter.

4.  Toss drained pasta with sauce. Serve immediately, sprinkled with Parmesan.

*— Il Fornaio —*
*San Francisco*

# Capellini with Tomatoes and Basil Sauce

**SERVES 4 TO 6**

**TIP**

Make this in summer when tomatoes and basil are at their peak.

| | | |
|---|---|---:|
| 1 lb | capellini, angel hair pasta or spaghettini | 500 g |
| 1 1/2 lbs | plum tomatoes, chopped | 750 g |
| 1/2 cup | olive oil | 125 mL |
| 2 tbsp | minced fresh basil (or 1 tsp [5 mL] dried) | 25 mL |
| 1 | clove garlic, crushed | 1 |
| 2 tbsp | olive oil | 25 mL |
| | Salt and pepper to taste | |
| 1/4 cup | grated Parmesan cheese | 50 mL |
| | Fresh basil leaves | |

1.  In a large pot of boiling salted water, cook capellini 6 to 8 minutes or until *al dente*. Meanwhile, prepare the sauce.

2.  In a bowl, stir together tomatoes, 1/2 cup (125 mL) olive oil, basil and garlic. In a large saucepan, heat 2 tbsp (25 mL) oil over medium-high heat. Cook tomato mixture just until hot.

3.  Toss drained pasta with sauce. Season to taste with salt and pepper. Serve immediately, sprinkled with Parmesan and garnished with basil leaves.

*— Il Fornaio —*
*San Francisco*

# Rigatoni with Roasted Tomato Sauce

**SERVES 4 TO 6**

**Preheat broiler or turn on grill**

| 10 | plum tomatoes | 10 |
|---|---|---|
| 1 lb | rigatoni | 500 g |
| 2 tbsp | olive oil | 25 mL |
| 1 tbsp | minced garlic | 15 mL |
| 1/2 cup | sliced mushrooms | 125 mL |
| 1/4 cup | fresh or frozen green peas | 50 mL |
| 1/4 cup | chopped fresh basil (or 2 tsp [10 mL] dried) | 50 mL |
| 1/4 cup | grated Parmesan cheese | 50 mL |
| | Salt and pepper to taste | |

1. Broil or grill tomatoes, turning often, until charred, about 15 minutes. Transfer to blender; purée. Set aside.

2. In a large pot of boiling salted water, cook rigatoni 8 to 10 minutes or until *al dente*. Meanwhile, prepare the sauce.

3. In a large skillet, heat oil over medium-high heat. Add garlic and cook until golden. Stir in mushrooms and peas; cook until tender. Stir in tomato purée; cook 3 minutes. Stir in basil and Parmesan.

4. Toss drained pasta with sauce; season to taste with salt and pepper. Serve immediately.

*— Anthony's —*
*Houston*

# *Basic Tomato Sauce*

| | | |
|---|---|---|
| **SERVES 4** | | |

| | | |
|---|---|---|
| 3 tbsp | olive oil | 45 mL |
| 1/2 cup | finely chopped onions | 125 mL |
| 2 | cloves garlic, crushed | 2 |
| 1 | stalk celery, finely chopped | 1 |
| 1 | carrot, finely chopped | 1 |
| 1/3 cup | dry white wine | 75 mL |
| 1 | can (28 oz [796 mL]) plum tomatoes, with juice | 1 |
| 1 lb | dried pasta of your choice | 500 g |

1.  In a saucepan heat oil over medium–high heat. Add onions, garlic, celery and carrot; cook until softened. Stir in wine; cook 4 minutes. Add tomatoes, stirring to break up; reduce heat to medium and cook 30 minutes, stirring occasionally.

2.  In a large pot of boiling salted water, cook pasta until *al dente*; drain. Toss with sauce.

*— La Sila —*
*Montreal*

# *Pasta Puttanara*

**SERVES 4**

| | | |
|---|---|---|
| 2 tbsp | butter | 25 mL |
| 2 tbsp | olive oil | 25 mL |
| 1/2 cup | finely chopped onions | 125 mL |
| 1/4 cup | finely chopped carrots | 50 mL |
| 1 | stalk celery, finely chopped | 1 |
| 3 tbsp | sliced black olives | 45 mL |
| 3 tbsp | sliced green olives | 45 mL |
| 1 tsp | drained capers | 5 mL |
| 1/4 tsp | dried basil | 1 mL |
| 1 | anchovy, minced | 1 |
| 2 cups | canned tomatoes with juice, puréed, or chopped fresh tomatoes | 500 mL |
| 1 tbsp | tomato paste | 15 mL |
| 12 oz | fettuccine | 375 g |
| | Salt and pepper to taste | |
| | Chopped fresh parsley | |

1. In a large saucepan, heat butter and oil over medium heat. Add onions, carrots and celery; cook until softened, about 5 minutes. Stir in black and green olives, capers, basil and anchovy; cook 1 minute. Stir in puréed tomatoes and tomato paste; cook 15 minutes, stirring occasionally.

2. Meanwhile, in a large pot of boiling salted water, cook fettuccine 8 to 10 minutes or until *al dente*; drain.

3. Toss pasta with sauce; season to taste with salt and pepper. Serve immediately, sprinkled with parsley.

*— Dalesio's —*
*Baltimore*

# *Rigatoni in Red Wine Sauce*

**SERVES 4**

| 1 cup | red wine, preferably Barolo | 250 mL |
|-------|------------------------------|--------|
| 2 cups | prepared tomato sauce | 500 mL |
| 1/2 cup | chopped onions | 125 mL |
| 1 | sprig fresh thyme (or 1/2 tsp [2 mL] dried) | 1 |
| 12 oz | rigatoni | 375 g |

1. In a saucepan bring wine to a boil; cook until reduced by half, about 4 minutes. Stir in tomato sauce, onions and thyme; reduce heat to medium-low and cook 15 minutes.

2. Meanwhile, in large pot of boiling salted water, cook rigatoni 8 to 10 minutes or until *al dente*; drain.

3. Toss pasta with sauce. Serve immediately.

*— Il Posto —*
*Toronto*

# Risottos

# Risotto with Fresh Spring Vegetables

| 2 cups | diced vegetables | 500 mL |
| 3 cups | chicken stock | 750 mL |
| 1 cup | prepared tomato sauce | 250 mL |
| 1/4 cup | butter | 50 mL |
| 1 cup | Italian arborio rice | 250 mL |
| 1/4 cup | grated Parmesan cheese | 50 mL |
| | Salt and pepper to taste | |

1. In pot of boiling water, blanch vegetables 1 minute; drain and set aside. In a saucepan, bring stock and tomato sauce to a boil; reduce heat to medium-low.

2. In a saucepan melt butter over medium heat. Stir in rice; cook, stirring, 5 minutes. Add 1/2 cup (125 mL) hot chicken stock mixture to rice, stirring constantly. Adjust the heat so the rice mixture is just bubbling; you don't want it so hot that the stock evaporates away as soon as you add it. When all the stock has been absorbed by the rice, add another 1/2 cup (125 mL) stock. Repeat procedure, stirring, until rice is tender, about 20 to 25 minutes; you may not need to add all of the stock mixture. Stir in vegetables. Remove from heat.

3. Stir in Parmesan cheese. Season to taste with salt and pepper. Serve immediately.

*Locanda Veneta*
*Los Angeles*

# Risotto with Mushrooms, Onions and Brandy

**SERVES 4 TO 6**

**TIP**

Use oyster or chanterelle mushrooms for an extra-special dish.

| | | |
|---|---|---|
| 2 tbsp | butter | 25 mL |
| 2 tbsp | olive oil | 25 mL |
| 1 cup | chopped onions | 250 mL |
| 1 1/2 tsp | minced garlic | 7 mL |
| 12 oz | mushrooms, chopped | 375 g |
| 1/4 cup | brandy | 50 mL |
| 1 cup | Italian arborio rice | 250 mL |
| 1 | bay leaf | 1 |
| 3 cups | hot chicken stock | 750 mL |
| 1/2 cup | grated Parmesan cheese | 125 mL |
| | Salt and pepper to taste | |

1. In saucepan heat butter and oil over medium heat. Add onions and garlic; cook until golden. Stir in mushrooms; cook until tender. Increase heat to high and stir in brandy; stir until liquid almost evaporated. Reduce heat to medium and stir in rice; cook, stirring, 5 minutes.

2. Stir in bay leaf. Add 1/2 cup (125 mL) hot chicken stock to rice, stirring constantly. Adjust the heat so the rice mixture is just bubbling; you don't want it so hot that the stock evaporates away as soon as you add it. When all the stock has been absorbed by the rice, add another 1/2 cup (125 mL) stock. Repeat procedure, stirring, until rice is tender, about 20 to 25 minutes; you may not need to add all of the stock. Remove from heat.

3. Stir in Parmesan; season to taste with salt and pepper. Serve immediately.

*City Restaurant*
*Los Angeles*

# Risotto with Sweet Sausage and Vegetables

SERVES 4 TO 6

**TIP**

Use bacon if pancetta is unavailable.

| | | |
|---|---|---:|
| 1/4 cup | butter | 50 mL |
| 1 tsp | olive oil | 5 mL |
| 2 oz | pancetta, chopped | 50 g |
| 1/2 cup | chopped onions | 125 mL |
| 1/2 cup | chopped carrots | 125 mL |
| 1 | stalk celery, chopped | 1 |
| 6 oz | sweet (mild) sausage, casings removed | 175 g |
| 1 cup | Italian arborio rice | 250 mL |
| 3 1/2 cups | hot beef stock | 875 mL |
| 1/4 cup | grated Parmesan cheese | 50 mL |

1. In a saucepan heat butter and oil over medium heat. Add pancetta, onions, carrots and celery; cook until vegetables are softened. Add sausage meat, stirring to break up; cook until no longer pink, about 5 minutes. Stir in rice; cook, stirring, until rice is coated and hot.

2. Add 1/2 cup (125 mL) hot beef stock to rice, stirring constantly. Adjust heat so rice mixture is just bubbling; you don't want it so hot that the stock evaporates as soon as you add it. When all the stock has been absorbed by the rice, add another 1/2 cup (125 mL) stock. Repeat procedure, stirring, until rice is tender, about 20 to 25 minutes. (You may not need to add all of the stock.) Remove from heat.

3. Stir in Parmesan. Serve immediately.

*Momo's Italian Specialties*

*Dallas*

# Risotto with Pine Nuts and Spinach

**SERVES 4 TO 6**

**TIP**

To toast pine nuts, bake in 350° F (180° C) oven about 8 minutes or until golden and fragrant.

| | | |
|---|---|---:|
| 1 | package (10 oz [300 g]) frozen spinach | 1 |
| 2 tbsp | butter | 25 mL |
| 1 tbsp | oil | 15 mL |
| 2 tbsp | finely chopped onions | 25 mL |
| 1 cup | Italian arborio rice | 250 mL |
| 3 cups | hot chicken stock | 750 mL |
| 1/3 cup | toasted pine nuts | 75 mL |
| 1/4 cup | grated Parmesan cheese | 50 mL |

1. In a small saucepan of boiling water, cook spinach until tender; drain. Squeeze out excess moisture, chop and set aside.

2. In a saucepan heat butter and oil over medium heat. Add onions and cook until soft. Stir in rice; cook, stirring, 2 minutes. Add 1/2 cup (125 mL) hot chicken stock to rice, stirring constantly. Adjust the heat so the rice mixture is just bubbling; you don't want it so hot that the stock evaporates as soon as you add it. When all the stock has been absorbed by the rice, add another 1/2 cup (125 mL) stock. Repeat procedure, stirring, until rice is tender, about 20 to 25 minutes. (You may not need to add all of the stock.) Stir in spinach and pine nuts. Remove from heat.

3. Stir in Parmesan. Serve immediately.

*— Galileo —*
*Washington*

# *Risotto Fiorentina*

**SERVES 4 TO 6**

| | | |
|---|---|---:|
| 2 tbsp | olive oil | 25 mL |
| 1 tbsp | butter | 15 mL |
| 1 tbsp | minced fresh basil (or 1/2 tsp [2 mL] dried) | 15 mL |
| 1 tbsp | finely chopped carrots | 15 mL |
| 1 tbsp | finely chopped celery | 15 mL |
| 1 tbsp | minced fresh parsley (or 1 tsp [5 mL] dried) | 15 mL |
| 4 oz | ground beef | 125 g |
| 1/4 cup | white wine | 50 mL |
| 1 cup | Italian arborio rice | 250 mL |
| 3 1/2 cups | hot beef stock | 875 mL |
| 1/3 cup | grated Parmesan cheese | 75 mL |

1. In a saucepan heat oil and butter over medium heat. Add basil, carrots, celery and parsley; cook 3 minutes. Add beef, stirring to break up; cook until no longer pink, about 5 minutes. Stir in wine; cook 2 minutes longer.

2. Stir in rice; cook, stirring, 5 minutes. Add 1/2 cup (125 mL) hot beef stock to rice, stirring constantly. Adjust the heat so the rice mixture is just bubbling; you don't want it so hot that the stock evaporates as soon as you add it. When all the stock has been absorbed by the rice, add another 1/2 cup (125 mL) stock. Repeat procedure, stirring, until rice is tender, about 20 to 25 minutes. (You may not need to add all of the stock.) Remove from heat.

3. Stir in Parmesan. Serve immediately.

*Toscano's Restaurant*
*Boston*

# *Italian Rice with Spring Vegetables*

**SERVES 4 TO 6**

**TIP**

Use thinly sliced ham if prosciutto is unavailable.

| | | |
|---|---|---:|
| 1 | zucchini, diced | 1 |
| 1/2 cup | chopped broccoli | 125 mL |
| 1/2 cup | chopped cauliflower | 125 mL |
| 6 | mushrooms, sliced | 6 |
| 4 | asparagus spears, cut into 1-inch (2.5 cm) pieces | 4 |
| 2 tbsp | olive oil | 25 mL |
| 1 cup | chopped onions | 250 mL |
| 4 | slices prosciutto, chopped | 4 |
| 1 cup | Italian arborio rice | 250 mL |
| 1/2 cup | white wine | 125 mL |
| 3 cups | hot chicken or beef stock | 750 mL |
| 1 | tomato, chopped | 1 |
| 1/2 cup | grated Parmesan cheese | 125 mL |

1.  In a steamer set over a pot of boiling water, cook zucchini, broccoli, cauliflower, mushrooms and asparagus until tender-crisp, about 5 minutes. Set aside.

2.  In a saucepan heat oil over medium heat. Add onions and prosciutto; cook until golden. Stir in rice; cook, stirring, 2 minutes. Stir in wine; cook, stirring, until it has been absorbed by the rice. Add 1/2 cup (125 mL) hot stock, stirring constantly. Adjust heat so rice mixture is just bubbling; you don't want it so hot that the stock evaporates as soon as you add it. When all the stock has been absorbed by the rice, add another 1/2 cup (125 mL) stock. Repeat procedure, stirring, until rice is tender, about 20 to 25 minutes. (You may not need to add all of the stock.) Stir in tomato and steamed vegetables. Remove from heat.

3.  Stir in Parmesan. Serve immediately.

*Ristorante Primavera*
*New York*

# *Mushroom and Chicken Risotto*

**SERVES 4**

| | | |
|---|---|---:|
| 2 tbsp | olive oil | 25 mL |
| 1/2 cup | sliced mushrooms | 125 mL |
| 1 tbsp | finely chopped shallots or onions | 15 mL |
| 1 cup | Italian arborio rice | 250 mL |
| 1/2 cup | white wine | 125 mL |
| 3 cups | hot chicken stock | 750 mL |
| 3 oz | diced cooked chicken | 75 g |
| 1/4 cup | butter | 50 mL |
| 1 tbsp | grated Parmesan cheese | 15 mL |

1. In a saucepan, heat oil over medium heat. Add mushrooms and shallots; cook 4 minutes. Stir in rice; cook, stirring, 3 minutes. Stir in wine; cook, stirring, until it has been absorbed by rice.

2. Add 1/2 cup (125 mL) hot chicken stock to rice, stirring constantly. Adjust heat so rice mixture is just bubbling; you don't want it so hot that the stock evaporates as soon as you add it. When all the stock has been absorbed by the rice, add another 1/2 cup (125 mL) stock. Repeat procedure, stirring, until rice is tender, about 20 to 25 minutes. (You may not need to add all of the stock.) Stir in chicken. Remove from heat.

3. Stir in butter and Parmesan. Serve immediately.

*— Palio —*
*New York*

# Cold Pasta Salads

# Linguine Salad with Brie Cheese and Tomatoes

SERVES 4 TO 6

**TIP**

Make this in summer when tomatoes and basil are at their peak.

| | | |
|---|---|---|
| 1 lb | tomatoes, diced | 500 g |
| 8 oz | Brie or Camembert cheese, diced | 250 g |
| 1 cup | olive oil | 250 mL |
| 1/2 cup | chopped fresh basil (or 1 tbsp [15 mL] dried) | 125 mL |
| 1/2 cup | thinly sliced sweet onions (Vidalia, Bermuda or Spanish) | 125 mL |
| 1/4 cup | grated Parmesan cheese | 50 mL |
| 2 tsp | minced garlic | 10 mL |
| 1 lb | linguine | 500 g |

1. In a large bowl stir together tomatoes, Brie, olive oil, basil, onion, Parmesan and garlic; set aside.

2. In a large pot of boiling salted water, cook linguine 8 to 10 minutes or until *al dente*; drain. Toss with tomato mixture. Chill 1 to 2 hours before serving.

— *Il Mulino* —
*New York*

# Pasta Salad with Black Olives and Feta Cheese

**SERVES 4 TO 6**

**TIP**

Substitute one small regular field cucumber if pickling cucumbers are unavailable.

| | | |
|---|---|---|
| 12 oz | small shell pasta | 375 g |
| 3/4 cup | olive oil | 175 mL |
| 8 oz | feta cheese, crumbled | 250 g |
| 3/4 cup | sliced black olives | 175 mL |
| 3 | kirby or pickling cucumbers, diced | 3 |
| 2 | tomatoes, diced | 2 |
| 1 | red onion, thinly sliced | 1 |
| 1/4 cup | chopped fresh oregano (or 4 tsp [20 mL] dried) | 50 mL |
| Dash | hot pepper sauce (optional) | Dash |
| | Salt and pepper to taste | |

1. In a large pot of boiling salted water, cook small shell pasta 8 to 10 minutes or until *al dente*; drain. Rinse under cold water and drain. Toss with 1/4 cup (50 mL) of the olive oil.

2. In a bowl stir together remaining olive oil, feta cheese, olives, cucumbers, tomatoes, red onion, oregano and hot pepper sauce, if desired.

3. Toss pasta with dressing; season to taste with salt and pepper. Chill before serving.

*City Restaurant*
*Los Angeles*

# Chilled Penne Tomato Salad

**SERVES 4**

**TIP**

Make this in summer when tomatoes, basil and peppers are at their peak.

| 1 lb | tomatoes, diced | 500 g |
|---|---|---|
| 1/2 cup | chopped fresh basil (or 1 tbsp [15 mL] dried) | 125 mL |
| 1/2 cup | olive oil | 125 mL |
| 1 | yellow pepper, thinly sliced | 1 |
| 2 | cloves garlic, crushed | 2 |
| 12 oz | penne | 375 g |
| | Salt and pepper to taste | |

1. In a large bowl, stir together tomatoes, basil, olive oil, pepper strips and garlic.

2. In a large pot of boiling salted water, cook penne 8 to 10 minutes or until *al dente*; drain. Toss with tomato mixture. Season to taste with salt and pepper. Chill 1 hour before serving.

— *Il Posto* —
*Toronto*

# Specialty Pastas

# Gnocchi with Meat Sauce

**SERVES 4 TO 5**

| | | |
|---|---|---|
| 3 tbsp | oil | 45 mL |
| 1 cup | chopped onions | 250 mL |
| 1/3 cup | chopped mushrooms | 75 mL |
| 2 | cloves garlic, crushed | 2 |
| 1 | carrot, finely chopped | 1 |
| 1 | stalk celery, finely chopped | 1 |
| 1/2 tsp | minced fresh rosemary (or 1/4 tsp [1 mL] dried) | 2 mL |
| 8 oz | ground beef | 250 g |
| 4 oz | ham, finely chopped | 125 g |
| 4 oz | chicken livers, finely chopped | 125 g |
| 1 tbsp | all-purpose flour | 15 mL |
| 1/2 cup | red wine | 125 mL |
| 1 lb | fresh or frozen gnocchi | 500 g |

1.  In a large saucepan, heat oil over medium heat. Add onions, mushrooms, garlic, carrot, celery and rosemary; cook until soft. Add beef, ham and chicken livers, stirring to break up; cook until no longer pink. Remove excess oil, if desired.

2.  Stir in flour until well-blended. Stir in wine and cook, stirring occasionally, about 20 minutes.

3.  Meanwhile, in a large pot of boiling salted water, cook gnocchi until *al dente*; drain. Toss with sauce and serve immediately.

*— La Riviera —*
*New Orleans*

# *Potato Mushroom Gnocchi*

**TIP**

Do not use new potatoes or baking potatoes for gnocchi, or the texture will not be right.

Keep cut pieces separate or they can stick together.

The cut pieces can be frozen raw and cooked later without thawing.

| | | |
|---|---|---|
| 1 1/4 lb | boiling potatoes, scrubbed | 625 g |
| 1/4 cup | olive oil | 50 mL |
| 1 tbsp | minced mushrooms, preferably wild | 15 mL |
| 1 tbsp | minced fresh parsley | 15 mL |
| 1 tsp | minced fresh basil (or 1/2 tsp [2 mL] dried) | 5 mL |
| 1 tsp | minced fresh rosemary (or 1/4 tsp [1 mL] dried) | 5 mL |
| | Salt and pepper to taste | |
| 2 1/4 cups | all-purpose flour | 550 mL |

1. In a saucepan add cold water to cover to potatoes; bring to a boil and cook until tender when pierced with a fork. Drain and peel. In a potato ricer or a food mill, mash the hot potatoes; set aside.

2. In a skillet heat oil over medium–high heat. Add mushrooms, parsley, basil and rosemary; cook 3 minutes. Stir mixture into mashed potatoes; season to taste with salt and pepper. Gradually add enough flour to potato mixture to form a smooth dough; knead, adding more flour as necessary, until dough is no longer sticky, about 5 minutes.

3. Divide dough into four pieces. On a floured board using your hands, shape each piece into a roll about 1 inch (2.5 cm) in diameter. Cut each roll into 1/2-inch (1 cm) pieces.

4. In a large pot of boiling salted water, cook gnocchi in batches until they rise to the top, about 4 minutes; carefully remove with a slotted spoon. Serve with your favorite sauce.

*— Palio —*
*New York*

# Crespelle (Crêpes) with Ricotta Filling

**SERVES 4 TO 5**

**TIP**

Use ham if prosciutto is unavailable.

## CRÊPES:

| | | |
|---|---|---|
| 1 1/2 cups | milk | 375 mL |
| 1 cup | all-purpose flour | 250 mL |
| 2 | eggs | 2 |
| 2 tbsp | melted butter | 25 mL |

## FILLING:

| | | |
|---|---|---|
| 1/2 cup | well-packed chopped fresh spinach | 125 mL |
| 1 cup | ricotta cheese | 250 mL |
| 1/3 cup | chopped prosciutto | 75 mL |
| 1/4 cup | mascarpone cheese or cream cheese | 50 mL |
| 1/4 cup | grated Parmesan cheese | 50 mL |
| | Salt and pepper to taste | |
| 1 | egg yolk | 1 |
| 1/3 cup | grated Parmesan cheese | 75 mL |
| 1/4 cup | melted butter | 50 mL |

1. Make the crêpes: In food processor or blender, purée milk, flour, eggs and melted butter until smooth. Heat a 9-inch (23 cm) nonstick skillet over medium-high heat. Using a 1/4-cup (50 mL) measuring cup, pour batter into pan, swirling pan to cover bottom with batter. Cook until golden on bottom, about 1 minute; flip and cook until golden, about 30 seconds. Repeat with remaining batter. Set crêpes aside.

2. Make the filling: In a saucepan of boiling water, cook spinach until tender; drain. Squeeze out excess moisture. Chop finely. In a bowl combine spinach, ricotta, prosciutto, mascarpone and Parmesan. Season to taste with salt and pepper. Stir in egg yolk.

*The Blue Fox*
*San Francisco*

3. Stuff the crêpes: Divide filling among crêpes and spread over surface of each. Roll each crêpe tightly into a tube. Cut each roll into 1-inch (2.5 cm) pieces. Put pieces vertically into a baking dish so filling is visible. Sprinkle with Parmesan cheese. Pour melted butter over top. Cover dish tightly with aluminum foil.

4. Bake until hot, about 20 minutes.

# Crespelle (Crêpes) Filled with Cheese and Spinach

**SERVES 4 TO 5**

**CRÊPES:**

| | | |
|---|---|---|
| 1 1/2 cups | milk | 375 mL |
| 1 cup | all-purpose flour | 250 mL |
| 2 | eggs | 2 |
| 2 tbsp | melted butter | 25 mL |

**FILLING:**

| | | |
|---|---|---|
| 8 oz | mozzarella cheese, cubed | 250 g |
| 4 oz | goat cheese | 125 g |
| 2 oz | blue cheese (preferably Gorgonzola) | 50 g |
| 4 oz | spinach, cooked, squeezed dry and chopped | 125 g |
| 1 tbsp | soft butter | 15 mL |
| 1 1/2 cups | prepared tomato sauce | 375 mL |
| 2 tbsp | soft butter or whipping (35%) cream | 25 mL |
| 1/3 cup | grated Parmesan cheese | 75 mL |

1. Make the crêpes: In food processor or blender, purée milk, flour, eggs and melted butter until smooth. Heat a 9-inch (23 cm) nonstick skillet over medium-high heat. Using a 1/4-cup (50 mL) measuring cup, pour batter into pan, swirling pan to cover bottom with batter. Cook until golden on bottom, about 1 minute; flip and cook until golden, about 30 seconds. Repeat with remaining batter. Set crêpes aside.

2. In food processor, combine mozzarella, goat cheese, blue cheese, spinach and butter; process until well blended.

3. Stuff the crêpes: Divide filling among crêpes and spread over surface of each. Roll each crêpe tightly into a tube. Chill rolls for 20 minutes. Cut each roll into 1-inch (2.5 cm) pieces. Put pieces vertically into a baking dish so filling is visible.

4. Pour sauce over crêpes. Put butter on top of tomato sauce. Sprinkle with Parmesan. Cover dish tightly with aluminum foil. Bake until hot, about 25 minutes.

— Centro —
Toronto

# Spinach and Ricotta Dumplings

**TIP**

These delicate dumplings will fall apart if the water is boiling, or if they are handled too roughly when removed from saucepan.

Instead of the butter-Parmesan sauce, serve with warm prepared tomato sauce and grated Parmesan cheese.

| | | |
|---|---|---|
| 6 oz | fresh or frozen spinach | 175 g |
| 1/2 cup | ricotta cheese | 125 mL |
| 3 tbsp | grated Parmesan cheese | 45 mL |
| 2 tbsp | all-purpose flour | 25 mL |
| 1 1/2 tsp | soft butter | 7 mL |
| 1 | egg | 1 |
| Pinch | nutmeg | Pinch |
| Pinch | salt and pepper | Pinch |
| 1/4 cup | butter | 50 mL |
| 1/4 cup | grated Parmesan cheese | 50 mL |

1. In a saucepan of boiling water, cook spinach just until tender; drain. Squeeze out excess moisture and chop.

2. In food processor combine spinach, ricotta, Parmesan, flour, 1 1/2 tsp (7 mL) butter, egg, nutmeg and salt and pepper; purée.

3. In a small saucepan, melt butter. Stir in Parmesan; set aside.

4. Bring saucepan of water to a simmer (do not boil). Drop dough into water by teaspoonfuls; cook just until they rise to the top, about 3 minutes. Carefully remove with a slotted spoon. Toss with butter sauce.

*Il Nido/Il Monello*
*New York*

# Capellini Frittata with Pancetta and Peas

**SERVES 4 TO 6**

**TIP**

Use bacon if pancetta is unavailable.

| | | |
|---|---|---|
| 2 oz | capellini, angel hair pasta or spaghettini | 50 g |
| 4 | eggs | 4 |
| 1 cup | shredded mozzarella | 250 mL |
| Pinch | salt and pepper | Pinch |
| 6 | slices pancetta, chopped | 6 |
| 1 cup | fresh or frozen peas | 250 mL |
| 1/3 cup | grated Parmesan cheese | 75 mL |
| 3 tbsp | olive oil | 45 mL |
| 3 | cloves garlic, crushed | 3 |

1. Break capellini into 2-inch (5 cm) pieces. In a pot of boiling salted water, cook capellini 6 to 8 minutes or until *al dente*; drain. Rinse under cold water and drain. In a bowl, whisk together eggs, mozzarella and salt and pepper; stir in capellini. Set aside.

2. In a skillet over medium-high heat, cook pancetta until crisp. In a saucepan of boiling water, cook peas just until tender; drain. In a bowl combine pancetta, peas and Parmesan.

3. In a large nonstick skillet, heat oil over medium heat. Add garlic and cook 1 minute. Pour half of the egg mixture into skillet. Top with pea mixture, then remaining egg mixture. Cook until egg mixture has set and frittata is golden on bottom, about 8 minutes. Turn by carefully inverting onto a large plate and sliding back into skillet. Cook until golden, about 5 minutes. Serve warm or at room temperature.

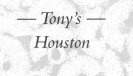

*— Tony's —*
*Houston*

# Low-Calorie Pastas

# *Penne Marinara*

**SERVE 4**

| | | |
|---|---|---|
| 1 1/2 tsp | olive oil | 7 mL |
| 1/2 cup | chopped onions | 125 mL |
| 1 1/2 tsp | drained capers, chopped | 7 mL |
| 1 tsp | minced garlic | 5 mL |
| 1 tsp | dried basil | 5 mL |
| 1/2 tsp | dried oregano | 2 mL |
| 1 | bay leaf | 1 |
| 1 3/4 cups | chopped tomatoes | 425 mL |
| 1/2 cup | sliced black olives | 125 mL |
| 4 tsp | tomato paste | 20 mL |
| 8 oz | penne | 250 g |
| | Pepper to taste | |
| 4 tsp | grated Parmesan cheese | 20 mL |

1. In a large saucepan, heat olive oil over medium heat. Add onions and cook until soft. Stir in capers, garlic, basil, oregano and bay leaf; cook 1 minute, stirring. Stir in tomatoes, olives and tomato paste; partially cover and cook 15 minutes, stirring occasionally.

2. Meanwhile, in a large pot of boiling salted water, cook penne 8 to 10 minutes or until *al dente*; drain.

3. Toss pasta with sauce; season to taste with pepper. Serve immediately, sprinkled with Parmesan.

*The Heartland*
*Illinois*

# *Linguine Toscano*

**SERVES 4**

| | | |
|---|---|---|
| 2 tbsp | olive oil | 25 mL |
| 1/2 cup | chopped onions | 125 mL |
| 4 | cloves garlic, crushed | 4 |
| 2 cups | canned tomatoes and juice, crushed | 500 mL |
| 2 tsp | dried oregano | 10 mL |
| Pinch | cayenne pepper | Pinch |
| 8 oz | linguine, preferably whole wheat | 250 g |
| 6 | black olives, sliced | 6 |
| 2 | tomatoes, chopped | 2 |
| 2 tsp | grated Parmesan cheese | 10 mL |

1. In a large saucepan, heat oil over medium heat. Add onions and garlic; cook until soft. Stir in tomatoes, oregano and cayenne pepper; cook 15 minutes. Meanwhile, in a large pot of boiling salted water, cook linguine 8 to 10 minutes or until *al dente*; drain.

2. Stir olives, tomatoes and Parmesan into sauce; cook until heated through. Toss with drained pasta. Serve immediately.

*The Heartland*
*Illinois*

# *Vegetable Lasagne*

**TIP**

Lasagne cuts into portions more easily if you let it stand 10 minutes before serving.

Ricotta is available in 5% and 10% M.F. (milk fat) versions — use the 5% to reduce fat and calories.

Prepare lasagne up to one day ahead. Store in refrigerator and bake before serving.

*The Heartland Illinois*

**Preheat oven to 350° F (180° C)**

**13- by 9-inch (3 L) baking dish**

| | | |
|---|---|---|
| 9 | lasagne noodles, preferably whole wheat | 9 |
| 12 oz | zucchini, sliced | 375 g |
| 1 tsp | olive oil | 5 mL |
| 1/2 cup | chopped onions | 125 mL |
| 3 | cloves garlic, crushed | 3 |
| 12 oz | frozen chopped spinach, thawed | 375 g |
| 1 cup | ricotta cheese | 250 mL |
| 3/4 cup | cottage cheese | 175 mL |
| 2 tbsp | grated Parmesan cheese | 25 mL |
| 1 tbsp | chopped green onions or chives | 15 mL |
| 1 | egg white | 1 |
| 4 cups | prepared tomato sauce | 1 L |
| 3 oz | mozzarella cheese, shredded | 75 g |

1. In a large pot of boiling salted water, cook lasagne 6 to 8 minutes or until tender; drain. Rinse under cold water, drain and set aside.

2. In a steamer set over boiling water, cook zucchini 2 minutes or until tender. Set aside.

3. In a saucepan heat olive oil over medium–high heat. Add onions and garlic; cook 4 minutes or until soft-ened. Stir in spinach; cook until liquid has evaporated. Set aside.

4. In food processor, purée ricotta, cottage cheese, Parmesan, green onions and egg white until smooth.

*Continued…*

RIGATONI WITH ROASTED TOMATO SAUCE (PAGE 133)  ➤

5. Assembly: Spread 1 1/3 cups (325 mL) of tomato sauce on bottom of baking dish. Arrange 3 lasagne noodles on top. Spread with half of ricotta cheese mixture. Top with all of spinach mixture. Spread with 1 cup (250 mL) tomato sauce. Top with 3 lasagne noodles. Spread with remaining ricotta mixture. Top with all of zucchini. Spread with 1 cup (250 mL) tomato sauce. Top with remaining lasagne noodles, spread with remaining tomato sauce, and sprinkle with mozzarella.

6. Cover dish tightly with aluminum foil. Bake until hot, about 45 to 55 minutes.

◄ PASTA SALAD WITH BLACK OLIVES AND FETA CHEESE (PAGE 147)

# Vegetable Cannelloni with Cream Sauce

**Preheat oven to 350° F (180° C)**

**13- by 9-inch (3 L) baking dish**

| | | |
|---|---|---|
| 16 | cannelloni shells | 16 |

**FILLING:**

| | | |
|---|---|---|
| 1 1/4 cups | finely diced carrots | 300 mL |
| 1 1/4 cups | finely diced onions | 300 mL |
| 12 oz | fresh spinach, trimmed, washed and coarsely chopped | 375 g |
| 1/2 cup | diced red or yellow peppers | 125 mL |
| 3 | cloves garlic, crushed | 3 |
| 4 oz | firm tofu, crumbled | 125 g |
| 1/4 cup | grated Parmesan cheese | 50 mL |
| 1/4 tsp | salt | 1 mL |
| 1/4 tsp | liquid smoke flavoring (optional) | 1 mL |
| | Pepper to taste | |

**SAUCE:**

| | | |
|---|---|---|
| 1 1/2 cups | chicken stock | 375 mL |
| 1/3 cup | finely chopped onions | 75 mL |
| 1 | clove garlic, crushed | 1 |
| 1 | bay leaf | 1 |
| 3/4 cup | 2% evaporated milk | 175 mL |
| 4 tsp | all-purpose flour | 20 mL |
| Pinch | nutmeg | Pinch |
| 1/3 cup | grated Parmesan cheese | 75 mL |
| 1 | clove garlic, crushed | 1 |
| | Salt and pepper to taste | |

**BREADCRUMB TOPPING:**

| | | |
|---|---|---|
| 1/4 cup | fresh bread crumbs | 50 mL |
| 1/2 tsp | olive oil | 2 mL |
| 1 | clove garlic, crushed | 1 |
| 1 tbsp | grated Parmesan cheese | 15 mL |
| 1 tbsp | minced fresh parsley | 15 mL |

1. In a large pot of boiling salted water, cook the cannelloni 10 to 12 minutes or until tender; drain. Rinse under cold water, drain and set aside.

2. Make the filling: Heat a large skillet sprayed with vegetable spray over medium-high heat. Add carrots and onions; cook until softened, about 3 minutes. Stir in spinach, red peppers and garlic; cook just until spinach wilts. Remove from heat. Stir in tofu, Parmesan, salt and liquid smoke flavoring, if using; season to taste with pepper. Stuff cannelloni shells; set aside.

3. Make the sauce: In a saucepan combine 1 cup (250 mL) of the chicken stock, onions, garlic and bay leaf; bring to a boil. Reduce heat, cover and cook 5 minutes. Remove bay leaf. In blender or food processor, purée mixture with remaining chicken stock; return to saucepan. Over medium-high heat, whisk in evaporated milk, flour and nutmeg; cook, whisking constantly, until mixture is bubbly, about 5 minutes. Stir in Parmesan and garlic; cook 2 minutes longer. Season to taste with salt and pepper; set aside.

4. Make the breadcrumb topping: In a skillet combine bread crumbs, oil and garlic; cook over medium heat, stirring, until golden. Stir in Parmesan and parsley.

5. Assembly: Pour half the cream sauce over bottom of baking dish. Arrange stuffed cannelloni on top. Pour remaining sauce over cannelloni. Cover dish tightly with aluminum foil. Bake 20 minutes. Uncover and sprinkle with breadcrumb topping. Bake uncovered until hot, about another 10 minutes.

# *Clam Lasagne*

**Preheat oven to 350° F (180° C)**

**13- by 9-inch (3 L) baking dish sprayed with vegetable spray**

| | | |
|---|---|---|
| 10 | lasagne noodles | 10 |
| 1 lb | fresh spinach, trimmed, washed and coarsely chopped | 500 g |
| 1 tbsp | margarine | 15 mL |
| 1/4 cup | all-purpose flour | 50 mL |
| 2/3 cup | clam juice or fish stock | 150 mL |
| 2 | cans (each 5 oz [142 g]) clams, drained and liquid reserved | 2 |
| 1/4 cup | chopped fresh parsley | 50 mL |
| 2 tbsp | lemon juice | 25 mL |
| 1/2 tsp | dried basil | 2 mL |
| 1/2 tsp | dried oregano | 2 mL |
| 1/2 tsp | dried thyme | 2 mL |
| 3 | cloves garlic, crushed | 3 |
| Pinch | pepper | Pinch |
| 2 cups | ricotta cheese | 500 mL |
| 8 oz | mozzarella cheese, thinly sliced | 250 g |
| 1/4 cup | grated Parmesan cheese | 50 mL |

1. In a large pot of boiling salted water, cook lasagne noodles 6 to 8 minutes or until tender; drain. Rinse under cold water, drain and set aside.

2. In a saucepan of boiling water, cook spinach just until tender; drain and squeeze out excess moisture; set aside.

3. In a saucepan melt margarine over medium heat. Stir in flour; cook, stirring, 1 minute. Whisk in clam juice and reserved clam liquid. Cook until sauce is thickened and bubbly, about 4 minutes. Remove from heat; stir in clams, parsley, lemon juice, basil, oregano, thyme, garlic and pepper.

*Canyon Ranch*

*Arizona and Massachusetts*

4. Arrange three lasagne noodles in bottom of dish. Layer with half the ricotta cheese, half the spinach, half the mozzarella cheese, a third of the clam sauce and three more noodles; repeat layers. Top with remaining clam sauce and Parmesan. Bake uncovered until hot and bubbly, about 30 minutes.

# Fusilli with Stir-Fried Beef and Vegetables

**SERVES 5**

**TIP**

Look for naturally-brewed soya sauce — it has a better flavor.

| | | |
|---|---|---|
| 1/2 cup | reduced-sodium soya sauce | 125 mL |
| 1 1/2 tsp | grated ginger root | 7 mL |
| 1 | clove garlic, crushed | 1 |
| 8 oz | fusilli | 250 g |
| 1 tsp | oil, preferably sesame oil | 5 mL |
| 8 oz | good quality steak, cut in thin strips | 250 g |
| 1 cup | broccoli florets | 250 mL |
| 1 cup | finely chopped carrots | 250 mL |
| 1 cup | sliced mushrooms, preferably oyster | 250 mL |
| 1 cup | thinly sliced onions | 250 mL |
| 1 cup | snow peas | 250 mL |
| 2 cups | bean sprouts | 500 mL |
| 1/4 tsp | pepper | 1 mL |
| | Hot pepper flakes to taste | |

1. In a saucepan bring 1 cup plus 2 tbsp (275 mL) water to a boil. Remove from heat; stir in soya sauce, ginger and garlic. Set aside.

2. In a large pot of boiling salted water, cook fusilli 8 to 10 minutes or until *al dente*. Meanwhile, in a wok or large saucepan, heat oil over high heat. Stir-fry beef until brown. Stir in sauce, broccoli, carrots, mushrooms, onions and snow peas; reduce heat to a simmer and cook 5 minutes, stirring occasionally. Stir in bean sprouts, pepper, hot pepper flakes and drained pasta; cook 3 minutes longer. Serve immediately.

*King Ranch*
*Toronto*

# *Fettuccine Alfredo*

| | | |
|---|---|---:|
| 1 1/2 cups | chicken stock | 375 mL |
| 1/2 cup | white wine | 125 mL |
| 1/4 cup | chopped fresh parsley | 50 mL |
| 2 | shallots, chopped | 2 |
| 8 oz | fettuccine, preferably whole wheat | 250 g |
| 1/4 cup | evaporated skim milk | 50 mL |
| 1 tbsp | all-purpose flour | 15 mL |
| 2 tbsp | grated Parmesan cheese | 25 mL |
| | Salt and pepper to taste | |
| 1 1/2 cups | chopped broccoli | 375 mL |
| 1 1/2 cups | chopped cauliflower | 375 mL |
| 1 cup | sliced mushrooms | 250 mL |
| 1/4 cup | fresh or frozen peas | 50 mL |
| 1 | carrot, thinly sliced | 1 |
| 1/2 | red pepper, thinly sliced | 1/2 |

1. In a saucepan bring chicken stock to a boil; cook until reduced by half, about 3 minutes. Set aside to cool.

2. In another saucepan bring wine, parsley and shallots to a boil; boil until reduced by half, about 2 minutes. Strain, discarding solids.

3. In a large pot of boiling salted water, cook fettuccine 8 to 10 minutes or until *al dente*. Meanwhile, in a saucepan combine cooled chicken stock, wine mixture, evaporated milk and flour; bring to a boil, whisking. Reduce heat to low; cook 3 minutes. Remove from heat and stir in Parmesan; season to taste with salt and pepper. In a saucepan of boiling water, cook broccoli, cauliflower, mushrooms, peas, carrots and red pepper until barely done, about 3 minutes; drain.

4. Toss drained pasta with sauce and vegetables. Serve immediately.

*Doral Saturnia*
*Florida*

# *Fettuccine with Sweet Peppers and Sun-Dried Tomatoes*

**Preheat broiler**

| | | |
|---|---|---|
| 1 | red pepper | 1 |
| 15 | drained sun-dried tomatoes packed in oil, cut in half | 15 |
| 2 | green onions, chopped | 2 |
| 1/4 cup | sliced black olives | 50 mL |
| 1 tsp | minced garlic | 5 mL |
| Pinch | pepper | Pinch |
| 1 1/2 cups | chicken stock | 375 mL |
| 3/4 cup | prepared tomato sauce | 175 mL |
| 8 oz | fettuccine | 250 g |

**SERVES 4**

**TIP**

It's more economical to buy dry-packed sun-dried tomatoes and rehydrate them yourself than to buy oil-packed. To rehydrate, bring a pan of water to a boil, add sun-dried tomatoes, reduce heat and simmer 5 minutes. Drain and use immediately, or put in a jar, add olive oil to cover, and refrigerate for later use. To reduce calories and fat, drain carefully and blot excess oil before using.

1. Broil pepper in oven, turning often, for 15 minutes or until charred. Cool. Peel skin, remove stem and seeds, and cut into strips.

2. Heat a large nonstick saucepan over medium-high heat. Add red pepper strips, sun-dried tomatoes, green onions, black olives, garlic and pepper; cook, stirring, 1 minute. Reduce heat to medium and gradually stir in chicken stock; cook 3 minutes. Stir in tomato sauce; cook until thickened, about 5 minutes. Meanwhile, in a large pot of boiling salted water, cook fettuccine 8 to 10 minutes or until *al dente*; drain.

3. Toss pasta with sauce. Serve immediately.

*Doral Saturnia*
*Florida*

# Pasta with Cheese Sauce and Vegetables

**SERVES 4**

| | | |
|---|---|---|
| 2 tsp | olive oil | 10 mL |
| 3/4 cup | sliced mushrooms | 175 mL |
| 3/4 cup | chopped onions | 175 mL |
| 1/2 cup | chopped green peppers | 125 mL |
| 2 tsp | dried basil | 10 mL |
| 1 tsp | dried oregano | 5 mL |
| 8 oz | fettuccine, preferably spinach pasta | 250 g |
| 1 1/4 cups | 2% milk | 300 mL |
| 1 tbsp | cornstarch or arrowroot | 15 mL |
| 1/2 cup | shredded Monterey Jack, Havarti or brick cheese | 125 mL |
| 2 tbsp | grated Parmesan cheese | 25 mL |
| | Paprika to taste | |

1. In a large skillet, heat oil over medium-high heat. Add mushrooms, onions, green pepper, basil and oregano; cook until tender. Set aside.

2. In a large pot of boiling salted water, cook fettuccine 8 to 10 minutes or until *al dente*. Meanwhile, in a small saucepan, heat milk over medium-high heat. Dissolve cornstarch in 2 tbsp (25 mL) cold water; stir into milk and cook, stirring, until thickened. Add Monterey Jack and Parmesan; stir until smooth.

3. Toss drained pasta with sauce and vegetables; season to taste with paprika. Serve immediately.

*The Heartland*
*Illinois*

# Linguine with Cheese and Tomatoes

**SERVES 5**

**Preheat oven to 400° F (200° C)**

**8-cup (2 L) casserole**

| | | |
|---|---|---|
| 1 1/2 cups | chopped plum tomatoes | 375 mL |
| 1 cup | shredded part-skim mozzarella or Havarti cheese | 250 mL |
| 1/2 cup | crumbled goat cheese (chevre) | 125 mL |
| 1/3 cup | finely chopped onions | 75 mL |
| 1/4 cup | grated Asiago cheese | 50 mL |
| 1 tbsp | mixed minced fresh herbs, such as oregano, rosemary, sage or thyme (or 1 tsp [5 mL] dried) | 15 mL |
| 8 oz | linguine | 250 g |
| | Salt and pepper to taste | |
| 1 | egg white | 1 |

1. In casserole stir together tomatoes, 2/3 cup (150 mL) of the mozzarella, goat cheese, onion, Asiago and herbs.

2. In a large pot of boiling salted water, cook linguine 8 to 10 minutes or until *al dente*; drain. Stir into casserole; season to taste with salt and pepper. Stir in egg white. Sprinkle with remaining mozzarella cheese.

3. Bake until hot, about 15 minutes.

*King Ranch*
*Toronto*

# *Pasta with Ricotta Cheese and Vegetables*

**SERVES 4**

**TIP**

Ricotta is available in 5% and 10% M.F. (milk fat) versions — use the 5% to reduce fat and calories.

| 8 oz | rotini, preferably whole wheat | 250 g |
|------|-------------------------------|-------|
| 1 tbsp | olive oil | 15 mL |
| 1/2 cup | sliced green peppers | 125 mL |
| 1 | clove garlic, crushed | 1 |
| 2 cups | sliced mushrooms | 500 mL |
| 1 cup | chopped broccoli | 250 mL |
| 3/4 cup | frozen or canned, drained corn kernels | 175 mL |
| 1 cup | cherry tomatoes, halved | 250 mL |
| 1 cup | ricotta cheese | 250 mL |
| 4 | green onions, chopped | 4 |
|  | Salt and pepper to taste |  |

1. In a large pot of boiling salted water, cook rotini 8 to 10 minutes or until *al dente*. Meanwhile, prepare the sauce.

2. In a large saucepan, heat oil over medium-high heat. Add green peppers and garlic; cook until softened. Stir in mushrooms; cook until tender. Stir in broccoli and corn kernels; cover and cook until broccoli is just cooked, about 5 minutes. Stir in cherry tomatoes, ricotta cheese and green onions; cook until heated through.

3. Toss drained pasta with sauce; season to taste with salt and pepper. Serve immediately.

*The Heartland*
*Illinois*

# *Angel Hair Pasta with Shrimp in a Tomato Pesto Sauce*

**SERVES 6**

*Cal-A-Vie
California*

| | | |
|---|---|---|
| 1/2 cup | white wine | 125 mL |
| 1 lb | shrimp, peeled and deveined | 500 g |

**SAUCE:**

| | | |
|---|---|---|
| 1 tbsp | olive oil | 15 mL |
| 1 | green pepper, chopped | 1 |
| 1 cup | chopped onions | 250 mL |
| 1 lb | mushrooms, chopped | 500 g |
| 1/2 cup | white wine | 125 mL |
| 2 lbs | plum tomatoes, finely chopped | 1 kg |
| 4 tsp | dried oregano | 20 mL |
| 1 tbsp | dried basil | 15 mL |
| 1 tsp | honey | 5 mL |
| 1 | bay leaf | 1 |
| 1 tbsp | tomato paste | 15 mL |

**PESTO:**

| | | |
|---|---|---|
| 2 1/2 cups | packed fresh basil leaves | 625 mL |
| 1/4 cup | walnuts | 50 mL |
| 2 tbsp | grated Parmesan cheese | 25 mL |
| 1 tbsp | olive oil | 15 mL |
| 3 | cloves garlic, crushed | 3 |
| 10 oz | angel hair pasta or capellini | 300 g |

1. In a small saucepan, bring wine to a simmer. Add shrimp; cook just until pink. Remove from heat; drain, reserving liquid.

2. Make the sauce: In a large saucepan, heat oil over medium–high heat. Add green peppers and onions; cook 5 minutes. Stir in mushrooms, wine and shrimp cooking liquid; cook 2 minutes. Stir in tomatoes, oregano, basil, honey and bay leaf; bring to a boil, reduce heat to medium and cook until thickened, about 20 minutes. Stir in tomato paste; cook another 10 minutes. Meanwhile, make the pesto.

3. Pesto: In food processor, purée basil, walnuts, Parmesan, olive oil and garlic until smooth. Measure out 1/4 cup (50 mL) of pesto for dish; refrigerate or freeze remainder for later use.

4. In a large pot of boiling salted water, cook angel hair pasta 6 to 8 minutes or until *al dente*; drain. Toss with shrimp, tomato sauce and pesto. Serve immediately.

# Pasta with Spinach and Seafood Sauce

**SERVES 4**

**TIP**

To make stuffing shells easier, carefully cut up one side with a pair of scissors; lay flat, stuff and roll.

| | | |
|---|---|---|
| 1 lb | shrimp | 500 g |
| 1 1/4 cups | chicken stock | 300 mL |
| 2 tbsp | rice | 25 mL |
| 1 | carrot, chopped | 1 |
| 1 | stalk celery, chopped | 1 |
| 1 | shallot or green onion, chopped | 1 |
| 1/2 cup | chopped onions | 125 mL |
| 1 | sprig fresh parsley | 1 |
| 1/4 tsp | dried thyme | 1 mL |
| 1 tsp | freshly squeezed lemon juice | 5 mL |
| 1 tsp | cognac (optional) | 5 mL |
| Pinch | cayenne pepper | Pinch |
| 4 | manicotti shells | 4 |
| 1 lb | spinach | 500 g |
| 1/2 cup | goat cheese (chevre) | 125 mL |

1. Peel and devein shrimp, reserving shells. In a saucepan combine shells, chicken stock, rice, carrot, celery, shallot, onions, parsley and thyme; bring to a boil, reduce heat to medium-low, cover and cook 25 minutes. In blender or food processor purée mixture. Strain it back into saucepan, pressing on solids to extract as much liquid as possible; discard solids. Stir in lemon juice, cognac (if desired) and cayenne; set aside, keeping warm.

2. In a nonstick skillet sprayed with vegetable spray, cook shrimp over medium-high heat just until pink; add to sauce.

*King Ranch*
*Toronto*

3.  In a pot of boiling salted water, cook manicotti 10 to
    12 minutes or until tender. Meanwhile, in saucepan of
    boiling water, cook half of the spinach just until wilted.
    Drain, squeezing out excess moisture; chop spinach
    and stir into goat cheese. Stuff drained manicotti
    shells with mixture. In a saucepan of boiling water,
    cook remaining spinach just until wilted; drain and
    divide among four plates. Arrange stuffed shells on top;
    pour sauce and shrimp over top. Serve immediately.

# *Linguine with Salmon, Leeks and Dill*

**SERVES 6**

## WHITE SAUCE:

| | | |
|---|---|---|
| 2 cups | low-fat milk | 500 mL |
| 1/4 tsp | nutmeg | 1 mL |
| Pinch | cayenne pepper | Pinch |
| 4 tsp | flour, preferably whole wheat | 20 mL |
| 1 tbsp | olive oil | 15 mL |
| | | |
| 1/4 cup | grated Parmesan cheese | 50 mL |
| 2 | leeks, thinly sliced | 2 |
| 1/4 cup | white wine | 50 mL |
| 2 tbsp | chopped shallots or onions | 25 mL |
| 2 | cloves garlic, crushed | 2 |
| 10 oz | linguine, preferably spinach pasta | 300 g |
| 12 oz | salmon fillets, skinned, boned and cubed | 375 g |
| 3 tbsp | minced fresh dill (or 1 tsp [5 mL] dried) | 45 mL |
| Pinch | freshly crushed peppercorns, preferably pink peppercorns | Pinch |

1. White Sauce: In a saucepan bring milk, nutmeg and cayenne to a boil; remove from heat. In another saucepan, combine flour and olive oil over medium heat; cook, stirring, until blended. Gradually add hot milk mixture, whisking constantly; cook, whisking, until thickened, about 5 minutes. Stir in Parmesan; set aside.

2. In a saucepan combine leeks, wine, shallots and garlic; bring to a boil, reduce heat and cook until vegetables soft, about 10 minutes. Meanwhile, cook the pasta.

3. In a large pot of boiling salted water, cook linguine 8 to 10 minutes or until *al dente*. Stir white sauce and salmon into leek mixture; cook just until salmon is barely done, about 3 minutes. Toss drained pasta with sauce, dill and pepper. Serve immediately.

*Cal-A-Vie California*

# Restaurant Profiles

The pasta dishes in this book were originally selected from the menus of top North American restaurants, adapted for home cooking, and published in 1991. The following profiles have been excerpted from that original publication. It is a fact of today's hospitality business that establishments come and go. And some of the restaurants described here have passed into gastronomic history. The recipes they inspired, however, like all those in this book, continue to stand as classics.

### ALLEGRO, Boston

In 1981, Jim and Bonnie Burke took a working-class bar and turned it into a dining room which served fine Italian food. Within 10 years, this Boston-area restaurant had diners lining up for its innovative cuisine.

### ANDREA'S RESTAURANT, New Orleans

The northern Italian food served here includes dishes that have been ordered by notables such as Queen Elizabeth and former President Jimmy Carter.

### ANTHONY'S/ TONY'S, Houston

The second of three restaurants (another being Tony's, also represented in this book), Anthony's is owned by Texas restaurateur Tony Vallone. With Chef Bruce McMillian, he has created a popular place where pastas are tender and desserts sumptuous.

### AVANZARE, Chicago

With its granite walls, bronze Virginio Ferrari sculptures, and bilevel dining room, Avanzare is itself a work of art. Northern Italian fare never tasted better than it does here, where the food has been simplified — pared down to its essence — allowing it to speak for itself.

### BIFFI BISTRO, Toronto

Biffi Bistro holds its place as one of the most popular spots in Toronto. With its open-style kitchen playing to the celebrity crowds, it offers relaxed but elegant surroundings. Named after a Milan bistro, Biffi introduced Toronto to sophisticated northern Italian cuisine.

### THE BLUE FOX, San Francisco

When Gianni Fassio bought The Blue Fox, it was like coming home. This restaurant had been in his family since the late 1940s, and Fassio spent most of his youth simmering soup. He gave up a prestigious accounting career to return The Fox to its days of splendor.

## THE BRASS ELEPHANT, Baltimore

The surroundings here are so beautiful you may never want to leave the dining room. Complete with hand-carved doors, a Moroccan teakwood balcony, and hand-carved ceilings and mouldings, The Brass Elephant offers rich, elegantly presented Italian food.

## CAFÉ DE MEDICI, Vancouver

Offering all the old-world charm and sophistication worthy of the Medici name, this restaurant caters to the classic northern Italian palate, serving elaborate food in a setting that is formal, yet warm and inviting.

## CAFÉ DES ARTISTES, New York

A former haunt of artists who lived and worked in Manhattan's Upper West Side in the early 1900s, Café des Artistes is a popular spot with celebrities. Its three-star menu is simply sumptuous.

## CAFÉ TREVI, New York

Down-to-earth food and a relaxed atmosphere make neighborhood patrons think of this restaurant as "their" place. Although the food is conventional Italian, it is so well prepared that you'll want to return.

## CAL-A-VIE, California

Tucked away in a serene setting, replete with colorful flowers on acres of rolling hills, this spa is a sanctuary for stressed-out America. The low-calorie cuisine boasts fresh produce from Cal-a-Vie's own garden.

## CANYON RANCH, Arizona and Massachussets

A haven for the overweight and over-stressed, Canyon Ranch offers a delicious menu developed by Jeanne Jones — author, syndicated newspaper columnist, and light cuisine expert. Canyon Ranch has two locations, both with views that approximate Shangri-La.

## CARLO'S RESTAURANT, San Rafael

A refuge from from sleek, trendy restaurants, Carlo's offers first-rate Italian food in an informal, out-of-the-way setting. The restaurant's emphasis is on quality; it uses the freshest of local ingredients.

## CENTRO, Toronto

Simple and elegant California-style Italian fare is the recipe for success at Centro. Ephemeral decor, a superbly stocked wine bar, and the latest in haute cuisine add up to a successful combination of ingredients.

## CHIANTI RISTORANTE, Los Angeles

Original wooden booths are reminders of the glorious past in Chianti, which may be the oldest Italian eatery in Los Angeles. Opened in 1938, it still offers some of the best classic Italian food in the town.

## CITY RESTAURANT, Los Angeles

At the forefront of American cuisine, Chef Susan Feninger's preparation technique is classic French, and her unique, eccentric menu features peasant food inspired by travels to Thailand, India, and Japan.

## DA MARCELLO, Montreal

Chef and owner Marcello Banini creates a new menu every night, preparing Tuscan food because "it's the most romantic." Banini travels back to Italy every year, looking for new recipes to bring home.

## DALESIO'S, Baltimore

Serving up up some of the best Italian food in town, Dalesio's proximity to Chesapeake Bay ensures fresh seafood. It also offers a spa menu — with no salt, refined sugars, or fat or cholesterol.

## DANIEL'S, Tuscon

One of the best Italian restaurants in the Tuscon area, Daniel's blend of old and new creates some intriguing cuisine. The decor is elegant, with separate dining rooms that are perfect for formal or intimate dining.

## THE DONATELLO - San Francisco

Classically inspired Italian cuisine abounds in this kitchen, with Chef Luigi Mavica paying tribute to Italy's regional foods. The extensive wine list is exceptional, and the two dining rooms are warm and intimate.

## DORAL SATURNIA, Florida

This lavish Florida spa is committed to healing both body and soul. The pasta, like *Fettuccine Alfredo* (page 167), has all the taste of a fine Italian dish, but is reduced in both calories and fat.

## GALILEO, Washington

Authentic northern Italian cuisine of the highest quality is served from this kitchen, resulting in some of the most inventive dishes in the city.

## GIULIANO'S, Carmel

This intimate, elegant restaurant serves superb food from the Negri family kitchen, where the motto is "a restaurant's food should stand on its own." Here, it always does.

## THE HEARTLAND, Illinois

Situated among the farmlands of Illinois, the emphasis at this exclusive spa is on relaxation and great food — low-fat, low-cal vegetarian, which is sure to do its part to help you reduce.

## IL CANTINORI, New York

At the door you are greeted by a colorful display of cold antipasti. A spacious restaurant, Il Cantinori nonetheless boasts an intimate feel. The menu is large and offers abundant choice.

## IL FORNAIO, San Francisco

Originally an Italian bakery chain with over 1,000 bakeries in Europe, Il Fornaio opened its first U.S. restaurant in 1987. As at the many others that have opened since, the bread and the food here are divine.

## IL MULINO, New York

Passionate fans wait patiently at the bar of this cramped eatery, even if they have reservations. Their patience is rewarded with wonderfully robust food redolent with garlic.

## IL NIDO/IL MONELLO, New York

Addi Giovanetti, one of the first restaurateurs to serve northern Italian fare in Manhattan and owner of Il Nido and Il Monello, is intent on pleasing your palate. Customer satisfaction is what these restaurants are all about.

## IL POSTO, Toronto

Consistency and superb quality attract an elite clientele to this northern Italian restaurant. Dishes are prepared minutes before they're served, and the homemade pasta is sauced seconds before it arrives at the table.

## KING RANCH, Toronto

Located on 177 acres of lush, wooded countryside, this spa offers cuisine that is light and satisfying and, with recipes like *Fusilli with Stir-Fried Beef and Vegetables* (page 166), never dull.

## LA RIVIERA, New Orleans

Chef Goffredo Fraccaro's travels to many countries shows in his inventive and imaginative cooking. He is the recipient of Italy's Oscar for Outstanding Achievement — the first ever presented to a chef.

## LA SILA, Montreal

Named after a mountain range in owner/chef Antoine Donato's home region of Calabria, La Sila attracts an eclectic group of patrons who come together for a taste of the exquisite.

## LA TOUR (PARK-HYATT), CHICAGO

A view of Water Tower Square through two-story-high windows set the scene for this culinary feast. Executive Chef Charles Webber has invented an exciting menu that will please the most demanding gourmets.

## LOCANDA VENETA, LOS ANGELES

Chef Antonio Tommasi, a native of the region of Veneta, cooks his distinctively regional cuisine in this tiny dining room. The open kitchen tantalizes the senses, transporting you to a different time and place.

## MICHELA'S, BOSTON

Owner Michela Larson works closely with her chef, creating exciting Italian fare for an upscale clientele. This popular Cambridge restaurant has received numerous awards for its hearty, country-style cuisine.

## MOMO'S ITALIAN SPECIALTIES, DALLAS

Owner/chef Antonio Gattini has been called the most authentic Italian chef in Dallas. His three restaurants attest to that skill, with Momo's boasting a large repeat business. Try *Spaghetti with Escargots* (page 81).

## MONTE CARLO LIVING ROOM, PHILADELPHIA

Here the northern Italian food is superb and holds its own against the sophisticated surroundings. Elegant waiters deliver attentive service, with ingredients presented at table.

## MOVENPICK, TORONTO

Steeped in old values like total customer satisfaction, the Swiss-based Movenpick chain has been extraordinarily successful. Here, chef Christian Aerni's fantastic creations lure both tourists and local diners.

## ON BROADWAY RISTORANTE, FORT WORTH

Hidden in a shopping strip, this bustling restaurant serves up moderately priced Continental Italian cuisine in a congenial atmosphere. Pastas are homemade, and the wine list is extensive.

## PALIO, NEW YORK

A private elevator conveys diners to this second-story restaurant, where they dine on owner/chef Andreas Hellrigel's ethereal food and partake of his world-class wine list.

## PAOLA'S, NEW YORK

Owned and operated by Paola Marracino, this tiny restaurant serves wonderful northern Italian food served in a warm, congenial atmosphere. Try the *Capellini with Asparagus and Scallops* (page 100).

## PRIMI/VALENTINO, LOS ANGELES

Valentino's ethereal food and Primi's tapas-style menu are testimony to the creative and bold approach Piero Selvaggio promotes in his restaurants. The pasta, which Selvaggio extols as a "universal" dish, is superb.

## RISTORANTE PRIMAVERA, NEW YORK

This uptown Manhattan Italian restaurant opened in 1979, and was one of the first to abandon the ubiquitous tomato sauce typical of that era. With its innovative dishes, the restaurant keeps diners coming back.

## SCOOZI, CHICAGO

Serving up trendy but good cuisine — with most items in servings large enough for two — this 300-seat trattoria is not for quiet conversation or romantic dinners, but the people-watching is superb.

## SPIAGGIA, CHICAGO

Homemade food, including pastas, is the mainstay of Spiaggia, a recipient of the prestigious Ambassador Award. Pasta dishes abound, with daily specials augmenting the already large menu.

## TOSCANO'S RESTAURANT, BOSTON

Chef-owner Vinicio Paoli, who trained in five-star hotels in Italy, consistently produces authentic Italian cuisine in an area where impostors of the "real thing" abound. The menu is short, but every item is superbly created, upholding the old adage that less is more.

## UMBERTO AL PORTO, VANCOUVER

Authentic Italian cuisine made Umberto Menghi's first restaurant a success in Vancouver in the days when spaghetti and meatballs were considered ethnic fare. Menghi is still working his magic at this pasta emporium. Fresh, reliable, inexpensive food is served in this converted Gastown warehouse, which boasts a congenial atmosphere.

## UPSTAIRS AT THE PUDDING, BOSTON

Serving out-of-the-ordinary Italian food, this restaurant, with its enigmatic name, is housed above the Hasty Pudding Club near Harvard Square. Chef/owner Deborah Hughes creates dishes grounded in traditional Italian cooking and filled with exotic ingredients from around the world.

# Index